11/10

D0116602

Eating Disorders

by Toney Allman

LUCENT BOOKS
A part of Gale, Cengage Learning

GALE
CENGAGE Learning

Detroit • New York • San Francisco • New Haven, Conn • Waterville, Maine • London

LIBRARY OF CONGRESS CATALOGING-IN-PUBLICATION DATA

Allman, Toney.
  Eating disorders / by Toney Allman.
    p. cm. -- (Hot topics)
  Includes bibliographical references and index.
  ISBN 978-1-4205-0225-1 (hardcover)
  1. Eating disorders--United States. 2. Women--Health and hygiene--United States. I. Title.
  RC552.E18A436 2010
  362.196'8526--dc22

                                          2009038864

Lucent Books
27500 Drake Rd.
Farmington Hills, MI 48331

ISBN-13: 978-1-4205-0225-1
ISBN-10: 1-4205-0225-5

Printed in the United States of America
1 2 3 4 5 6 7 14 13 12 11 10

Printed by Bang Printing, Brainerd, MN, 1st Ptg., 05/2010

CONTENTS

FOREWORD

Young people today are bombarded with information. Aside from traditional sources such as newspapers, television, and the radio, they are inundated with a nearly continuous stream of data from electronic media. They send and receive e-mails and instant messages, read and write online "blogs," participate in chat rooms and forums, and surf the Web for hours. This trend is likely to continue. As Patricia Senn Breivik, the former dean of university libraries at Wayne State University in Detroit, has stated, "Information overload will only increase in the future. By 2020, for example, the available body of information is expected to double every 73 days! How will these students find the information they need in this coming tidal wave of information?"

Ironically, this overabundance of information can actually impede efforts to understand complex issues. Whether the topic is abortion, the death penalty, gay rights, or obesity, the deluge of fact and opinion that floods the print and electronic media is overwhelming. The news media report the results of polls and studies that contradict one another. Cable news shows, talk radio programs, and newspaper editorials promote narrow viewpoints and omit facts that challenge their own political biases. The World Wide Web is an electronic minefield where legitimate scholars compete with the postings of ordinary citizens who may or may not be well-informed or capable of reasoned argument. At times, strongly worded testimonials and opinion pieces both in print and electronic media are presented as factual accounts.

Conflicting quotes and statistics can confuse even the most diligent researchers. A good example of this is the question of whether or not the death penalty deters crime. For instance, one study found that murders decreased by nearly one-third when the death penalty was reinstated in New York in 1995. Death penalty supporters cite this finding to support their argument that the existence of the death penalty deters criminals from committing murder. However, another study found that states without the death penalty have murder rates below the national average. This study is cited by opponents of capital punishment, who reject the claim that the death penalty deters murder. Students need context and clear, informed discussion if they are to think critically and make informed decisions.

The Hot Topics series is designed to help young people wade through the glut of fact, opinion, and rhetoric so that they can think critically about controversial issues. Only by reading and thinking critically will they be able to formulate a viewpoint that is not simply the parroted views of others. Each volume of the series focuses on one of today's most pressing social issues and provides a balanced overview of the topic. Carefully crafted narrative, fully documented primary and secondary source quotes, informative sidebars, and study questions all provide excellent starting points for research and discussion. Full-color photographs and charts enhance all volumes in the series. With its many useful features, the Hot Topics series is a valuable resource for young people struggling to understand the pressing issues of the modern era.

INTRODUCTION

IT IS NOT JUST ABOUT FOOD

Eating disorders are difficult to understand and difficult to diagnose and treat, but most of all, they are difficult to live with when they strike. Eating disorders are not choices or lifestyles or fads or teenage phases or weaknesses. They are dangerous illnesses that cause mental and physical suffering and may have lifelong consequences. People with eating disorders are unable to use food in a normal way—as a source of energy and nutrition. Their ability to connect hunger or fullness with appropriate meals is disrupted. Instead of enjoying a healthy diet, they are obsessed with food issues to the point that their feelings, thoughts, and activities are ruled by stress and worry about themselves and what they eat. Whether starving or compulsively eating or forcing their bodies to reject food, eating-disordered individuals are trapped in a pattern of unhealthy eating and emotional pain. The good news is that eating disorders are treatable and that people with these disorders can recover.

Most victims of eating disorders agree that the illness is not about food and weight. The pro-recovery Web site Something Fishy says, "They are just symptoms of something deeper going on, inside."[1] Although most experts suspect that people are born with the tendency to develop eating disorders, emotional issues ensure that the misuse and abuse of food persists, even when the victim wants to change. These issues may include self-hate, sadness, and feeling alone. Comments posted by eating-disordered people on Something Fishy reveal how much these emotions can hurt:

> As I'm smiling and laughing, I have voices screaming and degrading me in my head. I feel there's an empty hole in me.

> I believe that everyone's flaws should be accepted and forgiven except for mine.

> I wish that I didn't hate myself but at the same time, I don't know how it would feel to like myself.[2]

Individuals who suffer from eating disorders get trapped in an unhealthy pattern of eating to alleviate emotional pain.

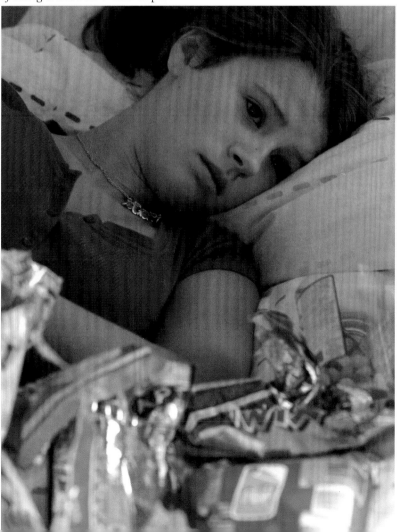

Recovery from an eating disorder means, in large part, facing and dealing with these bad feelings. Although it is painful and frightening, many people with eating disorders do find the courage and strength to fight their illness and do get better. They learn to like themselves, to eat normally again, and to lead fulfilling lives that are not ruled by an eating disorder. Something Fishy has an important message to those who are struggling to overcome these terrible illnesses: "If you have an eating disorder, you *can* find help. You *can* recover. And you *deserve* to do both."[3] The goal of scientists, researchers, and therapists around the world who work in the field of eating disorders is to find the best ways to make this recovery happen.

THE PROBLEM OF EATING DISORDERS

An eleven-year-old girl lay in a hospital bed. Although her name has been changed to protect her privacy, she is very real, as was her illness. Kelsey, according to her mother, was "only a handful of days away from death."[4] She had lost about half her body weight over a period of six months. Now she had heart problems, a very low body temperature, a brain that had grown smaller, and hair that was falling out in clumps. She looked like a skeleton. A feeding tube was pushed down her throat in order to get nutrition into her wasted body. Kelsey spent a month in the hospital before she was well enough to go home. Yet even then, her health remained in jeopardy because her mind rejected her body's need for adequate food.

Ben and Katie (full names also withheld to protect their privacy) were not as dramatically ill as Kelsey, but they, too, suffered physically because of their destructive relationships with food. Ben had asthma and was frequently hospitalized with serious asthmatic attacks that threatened his life. The attacks occurred so often because Ben's obesity exacerbated his breathing problems. Despite his fear and shame, he could not stop being a "compulsive eater" and would sometimes eat thousands of calories' worth of food at one secret meal. He said, "I think if I had had the guts, I would have killed myself."[5] Katie, a college student, did try to kill herself. Twice, she slit her wrists in an expression of self-hate and misery. Her desire to die was partially related to her frightening, uncontrollable habit of eating and then vomiting afterward to get rid of the meal.

Defining Eating Disorders

Kelsey, Ben, and Katie had eating disorders, as do approximately 0.6 to 4.5 percent of people in the United States. Some studies suggest that up to 24 million people in the United States have, or have had, an eating disorder. About 90 percent are females between the ages of twelve and twenty-five,

Eating disorders are seriously abnormal eating patterns that are both psychological disorders and medical illnesses.

but males develop eating disorders, too. Around the world, say experts, eating disorders generally affect young people living in developed countries that have achieved high economic status. Poor people in developing countries who are struggling to find enough food to survive do not develop eating disorders. Within wealthy societies, however, anyone of any class, ethnic group, race, gender, or socioeconomic status can be vulnerable to this disease.

DISTORTED BODY IMAGE

"One evening, I found [my son] looking at textbook photographs of concentration camp survivors. 'Can you see my ribs?' he asked, pulling up his T-shirt. Sadness ripped through me as I gently explained to him that he looked as thin as the victims in the pictures. His eyes filled with puzzlement. 'When I look in the mirror,' he replied, 'I see big rolls of fat.'" —"Mona," mother of an anorexic son.

Quoted in David B. Herzog, Debra L. Franko, and Pat Cable, *Unlocking the Mysteries of Eating Disorders*. New York: McGraw Hill, 2007, p. 151.

Eating disorders are seriously abnormal eating patterns that are considered to be both psychiatric disorders and medical illnesses that adversely affect physical health. Psychiatric disorders are emotional or mental problems that affect thoughts and feelings so that people behave in ways that are detrimental, disabling, painful, or unrealistic. With an eating disorder, these problems invariably lead to physical harm and suffering and sometimes even to death. An eating disorder is, therefore, a disease of both mind and body. The National Institute of Mental Health (NIMH) states, "An eating disorder is marked by extremes. It is present when a person experiences severe disturbances in eating behavior, such as extreme reduction of food intake or extreme overeating, or feelings of extreme distress or concern about body weight or shape."[6]

These extremes do not represent a conscious choice to eat too little or too much. A person who is overweight because of overeating or eating lots of fast food, for example, does not have an eating disorder, although his or her eating habits may be disordered. People whose diets are unbalanced because of frequent dieting in order to lose a little weight do not have eating disorders, either. Picky eaters or people who overdo sweet foods are probably perfectly normal. Even unusual thinness and obesity do not necessarily indicate a person with an eating disorder. Abnormal eating patterns may be unhealthy, but they are not true eating disorders. Eating disorders represent severe problems with food that dominate the victim's life. Although sometimes the disease may begin with a purposeful decision to diet or eat in secret, the disordered relationship with food soon spirals out of control. Eating disorders may take different forms, but they are real illnesses in which the victim has a distorted and disordered view of him- or herself. This view leads to unhealthy and dangerous eating habits that the sufferer cannot stop or reverse. Currently, eating disorders are defined by symptoms and behaviors as falling into three main types.

Anorexia Nervosa

Anorexia nervosa is the medical and psychiatric term for the disease of self-starvation. Although it can begin at any age, it typically affects adolescents and young adults. Experts estimate that anorexia occurs in about 1 in 100 to 200 young women, but about 5 to 15 percent of all anorexics are young men. "Anorexia" is a term from the Greek meaning "without appetite," while "nervosa" implies that the inability to eat has a psychiatric cause. People with anorexia actually do have an appetite. They simply are unable to give in to or respond to hunger and instead, severely limit their food intake. According to the National Eating Disorders Association (NEDA), anorexics exhibit four main symptoms:

- Resistance to maintaining body weight at or above a minimally normal weight for age and height.
- Intense fear of weight gain or being "fat" even though underweight.

- Disturbance in the experience of body weight or shape, undue influence of weight or shape on self-evaluation, or denial of the seriousness of low body weight.
- Loss of menstrual periods in girls and women post-puberty.[7]

David B. Herzog, Debra L. Franko, and Pat Cable, experts at Harvard's eating disorder treatment center, describe Shelley (not her real name), a thirteen-year-old who exhibited all four of these symptoms. Even though Shelley was not overweight, she decided to go on a diet. As she began to lose weight, she received a lot of praise from friends and family, but gradually they noticed that the weight loss did not stop. Shelley looked skinny

Anorexia sufferers have intense fears of gaining weight and often have to be hospitalized when their weight drops to starvation levels.

and unhealthy, yet her diet became more and more restricted. She displayed signs of anxiety and distress during family meals. Her father reported, for example, "Shelley would spread jelly on a slice of toast, scrape it off, and reapply it, repeating this process 15 times before she'd take a bite. It was agonizing to watch. I remember making pancakes for breakfast. Shelley put one on her plate, cut it up into miniscule pieces, and took more than an hour to eat them."[8]

Shelley demonstrated her fear of and resistance to weight gain in other ways, too. She began eliminating whole food groups, such as meat and sweets, from her diet. She lied to and tricked her parents about what she had eaten. For instance, she would arrange a bowl with a bit of milk and one or two flakes of cereal in it. She left the bowl on the kitchen counter in an effort to fool her parents into thinking she had eaten breakfast before leaving for school. She always told her parents that she ate at school, while in reality, she was skipping lunch altogether. She stopped going out with friends because their gatherings so often included having a pizza or hamburgers together. When she was forced to sit down at the table with her family, Shelley pretended to eat by raising her filled fork to her mouth, then, when no one was watching, lowering it still full, and by moving the food around on her plate. Herzog, Franko, and Cable explain, "The tendency to distort the truth, create false impressions, or lie about food intake is common among many with anorexia. Individuals describe a fear of weight gain so overwhelming that any perceived threat of losing control of the disordered behaviors becomes frightening, even unbearable. Therefore, patients resort to frantic efforts to continue their pursuit of thinness."[9]

Medical Issues

Despite being semi-starved, people such as Shelley are sure that they are too big. When they look in the mirror, they do not see "skin and bones" but fatness. Therefore, they are determined to deny any type of problem and insist (and believe) that they are eating healthily and need to lose more weight. Their body images, or how they see themselves, are distorted and because of this, they become more determined to restrict the foods they allow themselves. Eventually the types of foods and calories eaten become so limited that anorexics are seriously malnourished. The meals they eat are so tiny that their bodies cannot grow and develop or prevent the damage being done to their organs. Girls who allow themselves to become this malnourished will experience amenorrhea, or a complete cessation of their periods because their body fat drops so low.

Lack of menstrual periods, however, is but one of several medical complications of anorexia. In the face of starvation, muscles also waste away. If the individual is young enough to be still growing, bone development can be retarded and stunted. Osteoporosis is likely to develop also. This disease, which usually occurs in the elderly, is characterized by a loss of bone density. The thinning of bones leads to increase risk of bone fractures and subsequent disability that can last throughout life.

When malnutrition becomes severe, every organ in the body is affected. Digestive problems include slowed metabolism, delayed gastric (or stomach) emptying, and decreased intestinal functioning. People may experience constipation and bloating. One teenage boy, for example, was misdiagnosed with celiac disease (an inability to digest the gluten in wheat) because of

Children in Danger

In 2008 researchers in Australia discovered that anorexia is becoming more common among children under the age of thirteen, with some as young as six years old. These younger victims tend to be sicker than teens or adults with eating disorders. More than half of them already had severe medical problems by the time they were first seen by a doctor. They were seriously malnourished, had heart problems, and suffered very low blood pressure. Out of the 101 anorexic children in the study, 80 percent had to be hospitalized immediately. Half of those had to be fed through a tube to save their lives. The anorexic boys were even more severely ill than the girls because they had lost more weight. Fortunately, treatment worked well with these young patients. More than 70 percent had recovered after one year.

How Anorexia Affects the Body

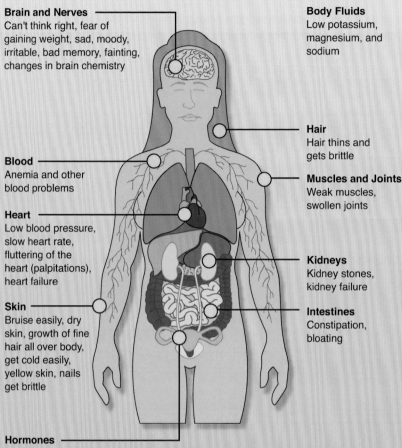

Brain and Nerves
Can't think right, fear of gaining weight, sad, moody, irritable, bad memory, fainting, changes in brain chemistry

Body Fluids
Low potassium, magnesium, and sodium

Hair
Hair thins and gets brittle

Blood
Anemia and other blood problems

Muscles and Joints
Weak muscles, swollen joints

Heart
Low blood pressure, slow heart rate, fluttering of the heart (palpitations), heart failure

Kidneys
Kidney stones, kidney failure

Skin
Bruise easily, dry skin, growth of fine hair all over body, get cold easily, yellow skin, nails get brittle

Intestines
Constipation, bloating

Hormones
Periods stop, bone loss, problems growing, trouble getting pregnant. If pregnant, higher risk for miscarriage, having a C-section, baby with low birth weight, and post partum depresssion

Taken from: WomensHealth.gov. Available at http://womenshealth.gov/faq/anorexia-nervosa.cfm.

his digestion problems before his anorexia was discovered. The brain and nervous system also suffer from malnutrition. As happened with Kelsey, cerebral atrophy—a reduced brain size—can occur, along with loss of memory, inability to concentrate, and even brain seizures. The body becomes unable to maintain a normal temperature, too, and the person may feel cold all the time. Hands and feet may turn blue. Hair loss and dry, yellow skin are common.

Perhaps the most dangerous complication of malnutrition is its effect on the heart and cardiovascular system. Pulse and blood pressure become very low. Eating disorder expert B. Timothy Walsh explains, "The pulse may be as low as 30 to 40 beats per minute, in contrast to the normal average of between 60 and 100 beats per minute—and changes in both pulse and blood pressure, such as what occurs when the person stands up, may cause dizziness and fainting."[10] The heart may deteriorate so severely that congestive heart failure develops, and death becomes a real possibility.

DAMAGED LIVES

"Eating disorders can have a profoundly negative impact on an individual's quality of life. Self-image, interpersonal relationships, financial status, and job performance are often negatively affected." —Academy for Eating Disorders

Academy for Eating Disorders, "Consequences of Eating Disorders." www.aedweb.org/eating_disorders/consequences.cfm.

Dangerous heart abnormalities can be exacerbated by other anorexic behaviors that are related to the urgent desire to lose weight and to hide eating patterns from other people. For example, people may use laxatives and diuretics in order to maintain a low body weight. Laxatives are meant to help people eliminate feces when they are constipated, but anorexics may use them in quantity to cause diarrhea and supposedly cleanse their bodies of "forbidden" calories. Diuretics (medicines used for increasing urination) are abused by some anorexics in order to get rid of water weight. Excessive use of laxatives and diuretics, however, upsets the body's electrolyte balance. Electrolytes are salts and minerals that help control the balance of fluid and conduct electrical impulses throughout the body. When these chemicals are out of balance, people are dehydrated and fatigued. Their muscles function poorly and since the heart is a muscle, heart rhythms become abnormal. If heart rates become too slow or erratic, hearts can stop altogether and death can result.

As a matter of fact, death rates for anorexia exceed those of any other eating disorder or psychiatric illness. Robert Levey, an eating disorder expert, reports, "Mortality associated with anorexia nervosa is high; 6-20% of patients eventually succumb to the disorder."[11] Fifteen-year-old "Michael," for example, was admitted to the hospital for his anorexia. Despite aggressive medical treatment, he was unable to correct the "vicious cycle" in which his brain could not receive hunger signals, and his body

Malnutrition causes cerebral atrophy. The dark red portion in this MRI scan shows an upper cerebrum that has atrophied.

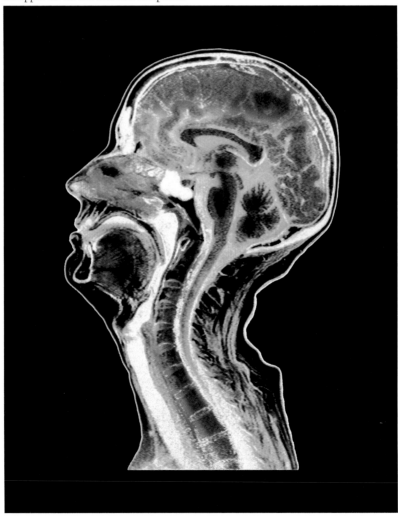

organs suffered "inexorable damage." Michael's doctor, Howard Markel, tried to fatten the boy with special milkshakes and put him on medication for depression. Nevertheless, once the doctor discharged Michael from the hospital, he began to starve himself again. Markel says, "Several months after Michael was discharged . . . the boy died . . . of a cardiac arrest." An autopsy revealed that Michael's heart was "wasted and shrunken."[12]

Michael's anorexia seemed to have been triggered by the death of his grandfather. The sorrow and fear Michael felt after he witnessed his grandfather's heart attack seemed to have pushed him into depression and anorexia. Depression is a factor in anorexia more than 90 percent of the time and can lead to suicide. Sometimes anorexic people are also perfectionists or obsessive and compulsive about behaving in the right way or doing the correct things. The desire to be perfect may lead to a need to punish oneself for "bad" eating behaviors. For instance, some anorexics force themselves to exercise extensively and work off any "extra" calories they could not resist eating. Others may be so upset about eating a "forbidden" cookie that they make themselves vomit afterward.

Bulimia Nervosa

Vomiting after a meal is considered a method of "purging" or "cleansing," and it is a factor in many cases of self-starvation. Vomiting is also a major factor in another type of eating disorder—bulimia nervosa. Bulimia affects perhaps 1.1 to 4.2 percent of all females—usually teens or young women. Fewer than 10 percent of bulimics are male, although in the last two decades the reported incidence in young men is increasing. People suffering with bulimia may not starve themselves, but their eating patterns are so disordered that they endanger themselves in other ways.

Bulimia is a disorder in which people are caught in a bingeing and purging cycle. NIMH says, "Bulimia nervosa is characterized by recurrent and frequent episodes of eating unusually large amounts of food (e.g., binge-eating), and feeling a lack of control over the eating. This binge-eating is followed by a type of behavior that compensates for the binge, such as purging (e.g.,

Bulimia nervosa is characterized by bingeing and purging.

vomiting, excessive use of laxatives or diuretics), fasting and/or excessive exercise."[13] A person with bulimia does not overeat, or binge, from hunger but because of psychological problems, such as depression or anxiety. The term "bulimia" comes from a Greek word that means "ox hunger" and describes a compulsive, huge appetite that may mean eating thousands of calories in a single meal. Then, the victim feels so ashamed, frightened, and disgusted by the binge that he or she must get rid of that meal. Most will vomit up the food, but many also exercise strenuously or use laxatives and diuretics to get rid of the calories. Just like anorexics, people with bulimia fear fatness and weight gain, but they usually are not emaciated and do not look starved. Nevertheless, they, too, can be very unhealthy.

Hayley (full name withheld for privacy) always thought she was fat, even though she was just a bit overweight at 5 feet (1.5m) tall and 125 pounds (56.7 kg). When she was in the tenth grade, she tried vomiting for the first time when going on a diet did not work. She was not losing weight quickly and was hungry all the time. One day, she says, "I went crazy eating too much food!" Hayley forced herself to vomit. She remembers, "It was scary, but I felt relieved. I figured this is great because I can eat whatever I want, and I can just throw it up later!"[14] Soon, Hayley was vomiting up to five times a day, and it became easier and easier to do.

Most people with bulimia force vomiting by sticking a hand or fingers down their throats to make themselves retch and gag. However, as time goes by many can vomit at will. Most, like Hayley, vomit several times a day and both binge and vomit in secret. Despite their fear and shame about their behavior, like anorexics, bulimics are unable to control their disordered eating patterns. They suffer from depression, self-hatred, and an overwhelming dislike of their bodies. They often know that their bingeing and purging is unhealthy but continue the behavior because of a fear of weight gain. They resist facing the true dangers of their disease. These dangers may not be as severe as the dangers of anorexia, but they are very real. The longer the bulimia continues the more likely bulimics are to develop medical problems and even life-threatening complications.

Lindsey Hall developed bulimia as a college student and suffered with the disease for nine years. She says she was "addicted" to her binges and explains, "I could eat a whole bag of cookies, half a dozen candy bars, and a quart of milk ON TOP OF a huge meal." She says that she ate so much during her binges that her stomach swelled up as if she were pregnant. After bingeing, she vomited. Eventually, her eyes reddened from the pressure of throwing up. The knuckles on one hand were rubbed raw from the long-term, repeated scraping against her teeth. She was physically exhausted, weak, and often dizzy. She was constipated and dehydrated. She adds, "Large blood blisters appeared in the back of my mouth from my fingernails. My teeth were a mess."[15]

Medical Issues

Dental problems are common for people who purge by vomiting regularly, and the majority of bulimics have cavities and eroded teeth. This happens because the acid in the vomit eats away the tooth enamel. Abrasions and calluses on the back of the hand that is used to trigger vomiting also occur in the majority of victims. The salivary glands in the mouth typically enlarge, and a person with bulimia may have puffy cheeks as a result. Dehydration and electrolyte imbalances occur in at least half of bulimic people, especially those who purge with laxatives and diuretics, along with vomiting. These people, like anorexics, risk heart

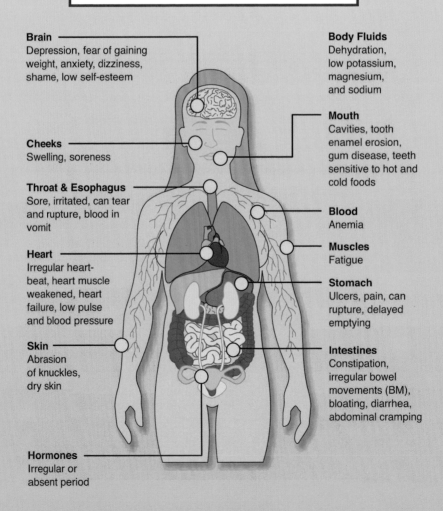

How Bulimia Affects the Body

Brain
Depression, fear of gaining weight, anxiety, dizziness, shame, low self-esteem

Cheeks
Swelling, soreness

Throat & Esophagus
Sore, irritated, can tear and rupture, blood in vomit

Heart
Irregular heartbeat, heart muscle weakened, heart failure, low pulse and blood pressure

Skin
Abrasion of knuckles, dry skin

Hormones
Irregular or absent period

Body Fluids
Dehydration, low potassium, magnesium, and sodium

Mouth
Cavities, tooth enamel erosion, gum disease, teeth sensitive to hot and cold foods

Blood
Anemia

Muscles
Fatigue

Stomach
Ulcers, pain, can rupture, delayed emptying

Intestines
Constipation, irregular bowel movements (BM), bloating, diarrhea, abdominal cramping

Taken from: WomensHealth.gov. Available at www.wwu.edu/chw/counseling/subpages/photos/bulimia.jpg.

The Bulimic Princess

One of the most famous modern eating disorder victims was England's Diana, Princess of Wales. In a BBC interview in 1995, she went public about her problem. She said, "I had bulimia for a number of years. And that's like a secret disease. You inflict it upon yourself. . . . You fill your stomach up four or five times a day—some do it more—and it gives you a feeling of comfort. It's like having a pair of arms around you, but it's temporary. Then you're disgusted at the bloatedness of your stomach, and then you bring it all up again. And it's a repetitive pattern which is very destructive to yourself."

Quoted in Susan Nolen-Hoeksema, *Eating, Drinking, Overthinking*. New York: Henry Holt, 2006, p. 23.

In 1995 Princess Diana admitted to having had bulimia earlier in her life. This picture from 1982 was taken during that time and clearly shows that she was very thin.

problems, irregular heart rhythms, and heart failure. Gastrointestinal complications can include tears in the esophagus from the strain of constant vomiting, chronic constipation, and bloating of the stomach. Occasionally, a life-threatening gastric rupture may occur. This means that the stomach may burst from a large binge, and this medical emergency often causes death. Usually, however, the danger of death is not as severe as it is in anorexia.

Binge Eating Disorder

Bulimia and anorexia share several symptoms, including depression and poor body image. Both kinds of eating disorders are extreme reactions to a fear of weight gain and fat, and both may include abusing exercise. Sometimes bulimic people fast and in other instances, anorexic people may purge. Another kind of eating disorder involves bingeing without purging. It is known as binge eating disorder, and it may be the most common of all the eating disorders. It seems to affect males and females about equally and perhaps occurs in about 2 to 5 percent of Americans. It occurs more often in adults than in teens or young people.

Binge eating, according to NEDA, is characterized by four main problems:

- Frequent episodes of eating large quantities of food in short periods of time.
- Feeling out of control over eating behavior.
- Feeling ashamed or disgusted by the behavior.
- There are also several behavioral indicators of [binge eating disorder] including eating when not hungry and eating in secret.[16]

People with binge eating disorder may be of normal weight, but they are usually obese. Along with obesity comes a serious risk of medical complications such as high blood pressure, diabetes, high cholesterol, and heart disease. The difference between typical overeating and binge eating disorder is that binge eaters have little or no control over their eating patterns. That is why binge eating disorder is sometimes also called compulsive overeating.

A woman who identifies herself as "Tracey" describes how helpless she feels about food. She says,

> There is never a time that I am not consumed with food. I'm either thinking about food, or eating. I work out regularly, and am quite busy so I appear to everyone else to be chunky rather than obese. No one has any idea how much food I eat, or how much I think about eating. I eat normally in front of people, and sneak the rest. I have

driven (by myself of course) to a fast food restaurant, ordered a large cheeseburger, fries and drink, eaten the entire meal in less than 5 minutes, then driven directly to a different fast food restaurant and ordered more. I will purposefully wrap all of the containers and bags up as small as I can and stop where no one knows me and throw the "evidence" away. . . . I eat until I feel ill. Many times if I am prevented from eating . . . I feel extremely angry and anxious.[17]

Many binge eaters feel depressed and disgusted with themselves after a binge eating session.

Stubborn and Poorly Understood Disorders

Binge eaters, just like people with anorexia or bulimia, are trapped by their emotions and their disordered responses to food. Their behavior is self-destructive, and yet they are powerless to do anything about it. That is why eating disorders are defined as both psychological and physical. They are psychiatric illnesses that are highly resistant to change or treatment and that may last for months or years with severe consequences for physical health. Eating disorder specialists, public health experts, and the medical community are extremely worried today about the lifelong damage that eating disorders can cause. Says the professional organization, Academy for Eating Disorders, "It is generally agreed that the incidence of eating disorders has increased over the last 30–40 years."[18] Yet no one really knows why eating disorders are becoming such a problem or what actually causes eating disorders or what should be done to reverse the trend.

THE CAUSES OF EATING DISORDERS

Only in the last couple of decades have society and medical researchers become aware of the widespread prevalence and dangers of eating disorders. So little attention was paid to the problem in the past that research into the "whys" and "hows" of eating disorders has not yet yielded definitive answers. Most experts today believe that different eating disorders probably have different causes and that a combination of factors is involved in the onset of eating disorders. Many scientists are convinced that the causes of eating disorders include psychological, genetic, biological, cultural, and social issues.

Gaining Understanding of Anorexia

Anorexia, although poorly understood and believed to be rare, has been medically recognized and described for hundreds of years. In 1689, in a British medical text, physician Richard Morton described two cases of anorexia, which he named "nervous consumption." At that time, consumption was the term for tuberculosis, because bodies wasted away and seemed consumed by the disease. Tuberculosis was known to have a physical cause, but Morton eliminated physical illness as a cause of the wasted bodies of his anorexic patients. He stated that the "nervous consumption" was due to "a multitude of cares and passions of her mind" in his eighteen-year-old female case. In the other case, a sixteen-year-old boy, he said the victim "fell gradually into a total want of appetite, occasioned by his studying too hard and the passions of his mind." Morton concluded "this consumption [was] nervous"[19] in origin, with the cause seemingly emotional and related to pressure and stress.

In 1689 British physician Richard Morton provided the earliest medical description of anorexia, calling it "nervous consumption."

Surprisingly, a case of self-starvation was not reported again until 1764, when physician Robert Whytt in Scotland described a fourteen-year-old boy who was sad, depressed, and unable to eat. Whytt identified the disorder as a wasting sickness. He wondered if the problem was in the nerves, the stomach, or the intestines. He explained that no physical cause for the disease could be found, and, therefore, no medical treatment was of any value. He frankly admitted that he did not understand the reason for the disorder.

Throughout the nineteenth century, anorexic illnesses were occasionally described by doctors but never scientifically researched. Generally, the medical community continued to see the starvation disease as a very rare psychological problem and referred to the cause as insanity, hysteria, or unsound mind. It was not until the twentieth century that anorexia captured the attention of the medical community and the public.

In the 1970s American psychiatrist Hilde Bruch claimed that in the recent past most professionals had learned about anorexia in medical school and yet never had seen a case for themselves. It was that rare. She went on to say that anorexia had "for the last fifteen or twenty years [been] occurring at a rapidly increasing rate." She explained, "New diseases are rare, and a disease that selectively befalls the young, rich, and beautiful is practically unheard of. But such a disease is affecting the daughters of well-to-do, educated, and successful families."[20] Bruch and most professionals of that time saw anorexia as a psychological problem which was the result of low self-esteem and poor body image caused by a culture that demanded perfection in women. It happened to "good," obedient girls who were afraid of growing up and unable to assert themselves to their parents or rebel in healthy ways. Perhaps because young people from poorer families could not afford to see a psychiatrist, Bruch did not recognize that the disease could afflict people from all classes and ethnic groups, but she did force the medical community to recognize the importance of researching anorexia and its causes.

Bingeing and Medical Knowledge

Bulimia was even less well known than anorexia until the twentieth century. It was not even recognized as a disease until 1979. Perhaps because people were usually of normal weight and kept their behavior secret, little is known about how the disorder was described in history. In the few cases that were medically described, bulimia was variously attributed to brain damage, intestinal worms, "hysteria," or "perverted appetite."[21] Not until the 1930s was bulimia recognized as an emotional illness or psychological problem, and not until the 1970s did the medical profession begin to report an increasing incidence of bulimia nervosa.

The Risk Factor of Growing Up

In 2007 psychologist Kelly Klump at Michigan State University reported that puberty seems to be a major risk factor in the onset of eating disorders, particularly anorexia and bulimia. Klump studied five hundred sets of female twins and examined the onset of their eating disorders. By mathematically analyzing when an eating disorder started and what happened with the other twin, she was able to conclude that eating disorders that began before puberty were caused by environmental factors. However, once puberty began, she said, genetic predispositions seemed to be activated and onsets of eating disorders dramatically increased in both sets of twins. As has been found with other studies, she reported that genetic influences seemed to be about 50 percent of the cause of eating disorders after puberty. Puberty is a time when dramatic chemical and hormonal changes take place as bodies grow to adulthood. Perhaps, suggest some scientists, these chemical changes activate the genes that predispose people to eating disorders.

Even then, it was defined as a special kind of anorexia caused by modern cultural pressure to be thin and beautiful.

Binge eating disorder also was rarely understood in the past. Although people with cravings for huge amounts of foods were written about in medical literature, no one saw binge eating disorder as a specific illness of extremes. It was not even recognized as an eating disorder until 1994. Before that time, professionals did not distinguish between obese people who were binge eaters and those who were not, although many doctors did believe that overeating was a symptom of emotional problems and depression.

Eating Disorders Are Brain Disorders

Today, scientists and medical experts recognize that emotional, psychological, and cultural factors may contribute to the development of binge eating disorder, anorexia, and bulimia. However, modern research suggests that these eating disorders are actually brain disorders. They are biological disorders caused by changes in the chemicals and/or the wiring in the brain that control information about appetite and eating behavior. Accompanying problems with depression and anxiety may be caused by these same chemical changes.

Serotonin in the Brain and Eating Disorders

Chemicals that help the brain send messages from one part to another are called neurotransmitters. One neurotransmitter is named serotonin. Psychologist Susan Nolen-Hoeksema explains, "Serotonin is important to the smooth functioning of many areas of the brain, including those involved with mood, appetite and eating patterns, and the ability to control our impulses."[22] Many people with eating disorders or depression have problems with the serotonin systems of the brain. Since the 1990s, studies have shown that people with anorexia have increased serotonin activity. Scientists believe that this disturbance in serotonin increases levels of anxiety and decreases appetite.

IT MUST BE IN THE GENES

"Arguments that social factors, such as girls feeling under pressure to lose weight to look like high-profile women in the media, contain logical flaws because almost everyone is exposed to them, yet only a small percentage of young people get anorexia. Those things are important but there must be other factors, involving genetics and science, that make some young people much more vulnerable than others." —Ian Frampton, pediatric psychologist at Great Ormond Street Hospital in London.

Quoted in *Herald Sun Australia*, "Eating Disorder Blamed on Genetics," March 31, 2009. www.news.com.au/heraldsun/story/0,21985,25264571-663,00.html.

In 2005 one group of researchers suggested that restricting food helps to lower anxiety by decreasing the high serotonin activity in the brain. The scientists said, "We hypothesize that people with [anorexia nervosa] may discover that reduced dietary intake . . . is a means by which they can reduce brain [serotonin] functional activity and thus anxious mood."[23] In other words, since anorexics feel better when they are less anxious, they are encouraged to eat less and less. Therefore, although this serotonin problem does not directly cause anorexia, it may make a person more vulnerable to the disorder. So far, only about half of the scientific studies of anorexics support this idea, but researchers continue to suspect that serotonin plays at least a partial role in the development of anorexia. Some studies suggest that serotonin levels are decreased in the brains of anorexics as a result of malnutrition, leading to depression and a loss of appetite.

People with bulimia also may have disordered serotonin systems. Scientists have long believed that people with depression have decreased levels of serotonin. Many researchers speculate that decreased serotonin activity in people with bulimia alters their mood, causes depression, and makes them feel the need to binge. Bingeing is soothing because serotonin activity is increased by eating sweet or carbohydrate-rich foods. Karl M. Pirke, an eating disorder expert, suggests, "Accordingly, binge eating might be regarded as a form of self-medication used to

This illustration shows a serotonin molecule with a nerve synapse in the background. Researchers think bulimics may have disordered serotonin systems.

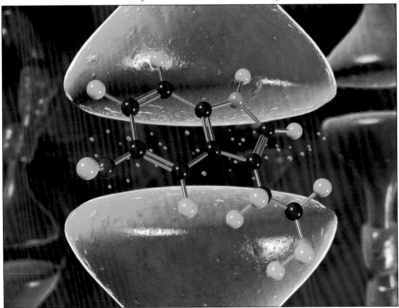

combat the negative consequences of diminished serotonin activity in the brain."[24] This same kind of self-medication also may be a factor in binge eating disorder, in which people binge without purging.

Dopamine and the Brain

Although many neurotransmitters are involved in brain activity, eating disorder researchers have focused mainly on two. Serotonin is the first, and the other is dopamine. Dopamine is involved in mood, attention, appetite, and learning. Researchers have discovered that when brains make too much dopamine, people can become obsessive, perfectionist, and worried. Too little dopamine can be associated with depression and an inability to enjoy experiences such as good food. Since people with anorexia are so often obsessive about food and diet, scientists suspect that dopamine may play a role in developing anorexia, too. Some studies suggest that anorexics make too much dopamine. The University of Maryland Medical Center states, "Recent research suggests that people with anorexia have increased activity in the brain's dopamine receptors. This overactivity may explain why people with anorexia do not experience a sense of pleasure from food and other typical comforts."[25] Anorexics may not need to seek pleasure from food since their brains are already producing excess dopamine.

Other studies point to decreased dopamine levels in eating disorders, especially bingeing—whether with purging or not. Bingeing activates the dopamine system, increases the pleasure signals in the brain, and eventually can create an addiction to food. The addiction happens because the brain loses its ability to regulate the dopamine system and becomes dependent on the food to get enough dopamine to make the binger feel good. Psychologist Caroline Davis at York University in Toronto, Canada, explains that binge eating disorder can be like substance abuse, only with fats and sugars. She says, "We are now getting evidence that excessive consumption of foods that our brains were not designed to cope with—high sugar and high fat—overtaxes these brain areas, contributing to a compulsion to have more."[26]

Hormones and Eating Disorders

The more scientists learn about neurotransmitters and eating disorders, the more they suspect that many chemical changes are involved in the diseases. Simona Giordano, an eating disorder expert, says, "It seems that multiple neurotransmitters are involved in eating disorders, but the neurobiology of eating disorders is not yet fully understood."[27] And neurotransmission is not the only brain function that may be involved in eating disorders. The hypothalamus is a small structure in the brain that plays a role in emotions (including releasing neurotransmitters such as serotonin), appetite, and sleeping, as well as producing hormones. Hormones are chemicals that control many body and brain functions. One hormone, known as cortisol, is a stress hormone and prepares the body to deal with threats and danger. Through a complicated signaling system that begins with the hypothalamus, cortisol, along with other stress hormones, is released from the adrenal glands. It helps initiate the fight-or-flight response that gets people ready to fight or run away, while it decreases, or turns off, appetite. This works well for short-term dangers, but when cortisol is highly increased for a long time and does not rise and fall normally, loss of appetite and depression can occur. Scientists have found that stress hormones, particularly cortisol, are chronically elevated in people with anorexia and bulimia.

Another hormone, known as leptin, is produced by the body's fat cells, travels to the brain, and is responsible for signaling the hypothalamus either to send out hunger signals or to recognize fullness after a meal. Leptin has been shown to be reduced in people with anorexia and bulimia. It has also been shown to be defective in people with obesity. Although people may have normal amounts of leptin in their blood, the signaling of fullness to the brain has been shown to work inadequately in both obese people and in people with binge eating disorders. Such people may not know how it feels to be full.

Brain Circuits

The ways that different areas of the brain and its circuits respond to stress also may be involved in eating disorders. For example, one 2009 study compared the brains of twenty wom-

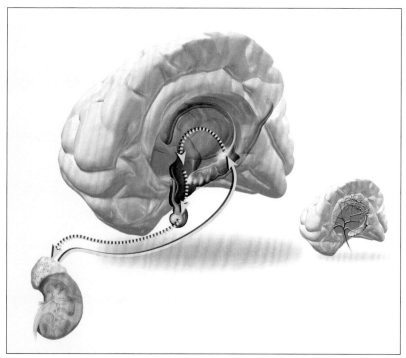

This illustration show the hypothalmus's (in pink) position in the brain and the hormonal pathways to the kidney. Scientists argue that depresssion may be caused by hormonal imbalances governed by the hypothalamus.

en with bulimia to twenty healthy women as they performed a frustrating, complex task. While the women worked, the researchers watched their brains in action using functional magnetic resonance imagery (fMRI). fMRI is a medical technique that allows scientists to measure the amount of blood flow in specific areas of the brain. Using a computer readout, researchers can see a detailed picture of the brain as it is working. In this study, the brains of the healthy women showed activation and increased blood flow in the areas responsible for self-control, self-regulation, and focusing attention. These brain areas activated much less in the women with bulimia. They responded impulsively to the task and made many more mistakes. The researchers concluded, "Self-regulatory processes are impaired in women with [bulimia nervosa], likely because of their failure to engage [brain] circuits appropriately." They speculate that this problem with self-control "may contribute to binge eating and other impulsive behaviors in women with [bulimia nervosa]."[28]

Studies such as this latest fMRI exploration are just the beginning in the attempt to understand how brain differences can cause eating disorders. Much more research needs to be done before scientists can know for sure the many biological factors involved in the development of all the eating disorders. Even then, a large question remains: What causes these brain differences in the first place? Many experts believe that the answer lies in the genes.

Genes That Control How the Brain Works

Genes are the basic units of inheritance in the cells of all living things. They are packets of deoxyribonucleic acid (DNA) that code for how an individual grows and develops. In humans, genes are arranged into twenty-three pairs of chromosomes, with thousands of genes on each chromosome. Although most genes in humans are the same for everyone, variations in some genes can determine whether an individual is at risk for certain diseases or vulnerable to environmental triggers of diseases. Scientists have found evidence that this is most likely what causes eating disorders. Binge eating disorder, for example, seems to run in families. James I. Hudson, a psychiatrist at McLean Hospital in Massachusetts, led a team that studied the families of three hundred obese people. Half of these people had binge eating disorder and half did not. The team interviewed family members and discovered that binge eating disorder was twice as common in family members of individuals with the eating disorder as in those who were not binge eaters. Hudson remarked, "This indicates that there may be a genetic component to binge eating disorder."[29] Anorexia shows the same kind of family pattern. One study demonstrated that family members are eight times more likely to develop anorexia if one member already has the disease.

Studies of identical twins support a genetic cause of eating disorders, too. Unlike fraternal twins or siblings, identical twins have almost identical genes. Scientists have discovered that when one twin develops anorexia, the other identical twin develops

The Singer Who Educated the Public About Eating Disorders

Until about 1983, almost no one in the general public in the United States had ever heard of eating disorders. Those who had heard of them were not really aware that eating disorders needed to be taken seriously. Even people who had eating disorders themselves often believed they were alone in their behaviors and had little idea of the dangers. This all changed when the popular singer Karen Carpenter died of anorexia in 1983. Suddenly the problem of eating disorders leaped into the public eye. Massive media coverage about her death and its cause scared people and forced them to think about the seriousness of eating disorders. Several celebrity sufferers came forward with their eating disorder stories and promised to seek help. Actresses Jane Fonda and Lynn Redgrave admitted to coping with eating disorders. Singer and actor Pat Boone admitted that his daughter had an eating disorder. Ordinary people, too, sought help for themselves or their loved ones with eating disorders. Many people say that Karen Carpenter's lasting legacy is the modern public's awareness of the dangers of eating disorders. Ironically, Carpenter had already sought help for her anorexia when she died. She was trying to eat and get healthy, but her heart had been too weakened by years of malnutrition to be cured.

Grammy-award-winning singer Karen Carpenter died in 1983 because of complications brought on by her chronic anorexia. Her death increased public awareness of eating disorders.

the eating disorder about 60 percent of the time. In nonidentical, or fraternal, twins this happens only about 10 percent of the time. So, it seems that at least 50 percent of the risk of anorexia lies in the genes. Scientists have searched for the specific gene that might be responsible, but as yet they have not been able to identify it with certainty. One gene that codes for reception of, or picking up, the serotonin messages in the brain has been most studied. Some studies found variations in this gene in anorexics, but other studies have not. Currently, scientists suspect that many genes are probably involved, but they do not yet know which ones.

Bulimia seems to have a similar genetic component. Studies suggest that when one identical twin has bulimia, the other develops it about 44 percent of the time. Researchers at Virginia Commonwealth University and the University of Pittsburgh Medical Center have been able to link bulimia to a chromosome known as chromosome 10. However, they have not been able to find the specific gene or genes on this chromosome that may be coding for a vulnerability to bulimia.

Pulling the Genetic Trigger

Even when the specific genes that code for eating disorders become known, however, scientists still will know only about half of the causes of eating disorders. After all, every person with an eating-disordered twin does not get an eating disorder. The other half of the cause of eating disorders is presumed to be in the environment, lifestyle influences, and personality. No one is doomed to get an eating disorder because of genes. Scientists generally think about genes as predisposing a person to developing an eating disorder but that something in the environment probably has to "pull the trigger." Medical expert B. Timothy Walsh explains, "It does not appear that eating disorders have a single cause; rather, multiple influences, called 'risk factors,' seem to combine and interact to eventually result in the occurrence of anorexia nervosa or bulimia nervosa."[30] The same is no doubt true for binge eating disorder as well.

The National Eating Disorders Association (NEDA) states that eating disorders can involve psychological factors, "interpersonal" factors, and social factors. The organization says, "People with eating disorders often use food and the control of food in an attempt to compensate for feelings and emotions that may otherwise seem overwhelming. For some, dieting, bingeing, and purging may begin as a way to cope with painful emotions and to feel in control of one's life."[31]

Psychological Risk Factors

The feelings and emotions NEDA describes as risk factors include low self-esteem (which means not valuing or thinking well of oneself), feelings of lack of control, and being depressed, anxious, sad, or lonely. No one knows why some people with low self-esteem fall into an eating disorder pattern while most do not. Nor have researchers been able to discover why depression, stress, or loneliness increases the risk for an eating disorder in some people but not others, except by assuming a genetic predisposition. Scientists have not been able to explain what triggers the eating disorder as a response to psychological problems. They do know, however, that these emotional difficulties can be found in almost everyone with any kind of eating disorder.

"NOT MY FAULT"

"I am relieved to know that this disease is not my fault, rather a complex combination of cultural influences, but more importantly those of genetics and brain chemistry." —Mia Prensky, bulimia sufferer.

Mia Prensky, "Bulimia on the Brain," *Serendip*, Bryn Mawr College, April 18, 2007. http://serendip.brynmawr.edu/exchange/node/371.

No matter what the eating disorder, people describe feeling very bad about themselves, having thoughts of sadness and suicide, and being anxious or stressed much of the time. Some researchers suggest that these feelings are a result of the eating disorders, not the cause. However, other scientists point out that problems such as depression seem to be caused by variations

Many young woman with eating disorders and subsequent low self-esteem see a distorted view of their bodies.

in chemicals in the brain, just as eating disorders are. People plagued with eating disorders may be genetically predisposed to depression, anxiety, and poor self-image. Some scientific studies of people who have recovered from eating disorders reveal that the psychological issues remain, even when the eating disorder no longer exists. Other studies suggest that personality and self-image can become normal and healthy when eating disorders are resolved. For now, all scientists can do is caution that these psychological issues are warning signs of an increased risk for eating disorders.

Interpersonal Risk Factors

Interpersonal issues may be one cause of developing emotional and psychological problems. How an individual is treated by other people can have negative emotional consequences. For example, people who have been teased, bullied, or criticized about their weight or appearance are at increased risk for an eating disorder. Troubled families also may cause the risk to increase. Expert Dermot J. Hurley suggests that the parents of teens with anorexia and bulimia tend to be overprotective, strict, and achievement oriented. They discourage displays of anger or rebellion in their children and emphasize cooperation, obedience, and striving for perfection. Hurley says, "These disorders [in the family] trigger bizarre and unique attempts by young persons to establish a degree of autonomy [independence and freedom] and control through food in an effort to maintain some sense of personhood and self-efficacy."[32] However, Hurley also points out that no scientific evidence supports the idea that dysfunctional families are a risk factor for eating disorders. He explains that experts have observed the negative behaviors of the families, but they cannot prove that family problems are a cause of eating disorders. The families may be disordered as a result of extreme worry about the eating disorder rather than having caused the eating disorder. No one knows for sure whether family behaviors are a true risk factor.

One family behavior, however, is known to be a factor in the development of eating disorders. Child abuse, both physical and sexual, can be a real risk factor for an eating disorder. In 2008 an Australian study of teens and adults with eating disorders found evidence of sexual abuse in one out of every two young women with bulimia. This compares to a one in five sexual abuse incidence in the Australian community at large. Head researcher George Patton says, "So the message is one of sensitivity to the possibility of past sexual abuse in young bulimic patients."[33] He speculates that the bulimia is a way of dealing with emotional distress. Patton and his team did not find the same link with sexual abuse and anorexia, but some other researchers have. At the respected Web site for eating disorders named Something

Children can develop an eating disorder due to both physical and sexual abuse.

Fishy, a poll was conducted of people with eating disorders. The poll revealed that out of two thousand people who responded, more than 50 percent reported suffering some kind of abuse during childhood.

Social Risk Factors

Polls are not always scientific, and studies of abuse as a risk factor yield contradictory results. Most experts say that the majority of people with an eating disorder have not been abused. Abuse is simply one possible risk factor. Everyone, however, is exposed to the social factors that may contribute to eating disorders. NEDA describes these factors as:

- Cultural pressures that glorify "thinness" and place value on obtaining the "perfect body."
- Narrow definitions of beauty that include only women and men of specific body weights and shapes.
- Cultural norms that value people on the basis of physical appearance and not inner qualities and strengths.[34]

Again, not everyone who wants to be thin and beautiful or who dislikes his or her body develops an eating disorder. But modern society's pressure to achieve a certain body type can lead to a desire to diet and get thin or to a need to exercise so as to be the perfect shape or, conversely, to a feeling of hopelessness about one's body. These feelings, in turn, can be risk factors for developing an eating disorder. Nolen-Hoeksema says that society and culture today have created a "toxic atmosphere"[35] in which eating disorders affect more and more people at younger and younger ages.

LIVING WITH AN EATING DISORDER

Everyone with an eating disorder is a unique individual with his or her own story to tell. Yet almost all, in one way or another, are powerless to make the choice to end the eating disorder. "Feeling out of control and overwhelmed, they experience a 'monster-like' force inside them that insists they maintain their eating disorder,"[36] explain experts Jane Shure and Beth Weinstock. No matter what the eating disorder, the individual suffers and feels taken over by the monster that will not let go.

Anorexia and Annaclaire

Annaclaire (full name withheld for her privacy) had always been a perfectionist, but her parents did not have much time to notice her worries. Her father was in the military and often moved from base to base in different parts of the world. Annaclaire and her siblings were sent to boarding schools. Annaclaire just wanted to fit in with the other girls. At the age of ten, lonely and vulnerable, she desperately searched for friends who would accept her. She found them in some older girls at school, who were constantly dieting and talking about their weight. Annaclaire remembers, "I worshipped the ground they walked on and decided that what I need to do to become like them was to do exactly what they did." She began to seek the perfect, thin body. First, the young girl started skipping snack time; then she began eating only half her breakfast; then she gave up lunch altogether. When she joined gymnastics and had to wear a leotard, she became even more weight conscious. She says, "I worried I was chubby, I worried I had cellulite, I worried that my thighs would jiggle when I competed."[37]

By the time she was twelve years old, Annaclaire was counting every calorie that went in her mouth. She also moved to a new boarding school. There, she quickly made friends with a fifteen-year-old anorexic girl who was known as the "diet queen." The two girls encouraged each other and made each other worse. Says Annaclaire, "With a partner in crime I learned everything I could about anorexia. I did my homework, read all the books, went to all the websites, devoured magazines with ED [eating disorder] articles, and became somewhat of an expert. I wouldn't say that it was a conscious decision to become an anorectic, but it's something I had considered. It just kinda happened."[38]

Anorexia sufferers will do excessive exercising like running as well as constant dieting in an effort to take off more weight.

Gradually, Annaclaire began giving up more and more kinds of foods. She would not eat pork or steak. She gave up desserts and sodas. She refused to eat casseroles or sauces because she could not tell how many calories were in them. She stopped eating breads and cereals. As her diet became more restricted, she began extreme exercising. She joined gymnastics and tennis and also began to run every morning. By the time she was sixteen years old, she lived by a rigid, self-destructive routine. In a typical day, Annaclaire ate half an apple and juice for breakfast; a skinless chicken breast, carrot sticks, and water for lunch; and a small, dry salad and perhaps a little of the school's main dish for supper. She ran 5 miles (8km) every morning and again each night. Her weight dropped to 80 pounds (36kg) and yet, she says, "I thought I was fine, I was just being healthy."[39] She continued to worry also that she was too fat.

A Body Pushed Too Far

Annaclaire transferred to yet another boarding school and increased the severity of her diet and exercise. She began to have fainting spells. As the adults in her life became concerned about her health, she remembers, "I said I didn't have time to eat; I thought I didn't need to eat." Finally, her parents had to come and take her to a hospital. Annaclaire had developed heart rhythm problems, muscle spasms, and pneumonia. In the hospital, she got scared and put on a little weight, but the improvement did not last. Back at boarding school, she dieted again, but she made an effort to keep her weight just high enough that her parents and teachers would leave her alone. She remained terribly underweight and began worrying about her feelings and emotions. She remembers wondering anxiously, "Was I OK? Was I happy? Why am I not happy? Is there something wrong with me for not being happy? Look at that girl, she looks happy, why can't I be like her? Why am I not happy, dammit?"[40]

It was not until Annaclaire went to college, endured another hospitalization, and returned to "insane exercising" to drop to 70 pounds (32kg) that she realized she was in terrible trouble and needed help. After many years of anorexia, she finally understood that an eating disorder "is no way to live; it's a way to die."[41]

Patrick's Anorexia

This realization comes to different people in different ways, if at all, and even then the anorexia does not stop. Fighting the monster inside is a constant struggle in which facing the problem is but the first step. Annaclaire got there without the support of her family. Patrick Bergstrom also had to make that first step alone, even though he had a very loving, supportive family. Bergstrom, too, had anorexia, but dieting did not trigger it—failure did.

Throughout his childhood, Bergstrom was a devoted athlete. By the time he reached high school, he was a star varsity lacrosse player. He was small for an athlete at 5 feet 6 inches (1.7m) tall and 135 pounds (61kg), but he was dedicated. Through willpower, hard work, and a determination to be perfect, he made himself into an accomplished, successful player and became "the all-time leading scorer" in his high school's history. He remembers, "Lacrosse soon became my life and my identity."[42] He was strong, healthy, competitive, and in love with his sport. He was happy with himself, and it never occurred to him that he could fail.

Patrick Bergstrom started an eating disorders blog and support group as part of his effort to cope with anorexia.

In college, however, Bergstrom's athletic career began to fall apart. He says, "All I had ever experienced up to this point was success and glory. I had never been injured and hardly spent anytime on the bench. I had never experienced failure nor did I know what it felt like." Bergstrom's favorite coach died in a sudden tragic accident. Bergstrom himself suffered knee injuries and two concussions. No matter how hard he trained and practiced, his new coach did not think he was strong enough or fast enough. Bergstrom often sat out games on the bench. He did not even get to play in the last game of his college career. He was so bitter and upset that he vowed never to play lacrosse again. He says, "I turned my back on the one thing I loved because I felt it betrayed me."[43]

After graduating from college, Bergstrom faced more failures that he did not know how to handle, and he did not have athletics anymore to help him work out the pain. He had a hard time finding a job and ended up with one he disliked. He started soothing himself by bingeing on alcohol and eating less and less. Then, he remembers, "Eventually, I got to the point that I would purge after eating to cope with the stress." His weight dropped, his substance abuse worsened, and the girlfriend he loved left him. Bergstrom went home to his parents who helped him to get treatment for his alcohol abuse, but the treatment did not help his eating disorder. Bergstrom did not even realize that he had one because he thought "this was something only women suffered from."[44]

Bergstrom stopped drinking but continued to feel desperate to become a success. He got back together with his girlfriend, began planning a wedding, and became a hard-driving "workaholic" at the office. Meanwhile, he was exhausted and in emotional pain. His anorexia grew out of control. As he ate less and less, he began to reject and withdraw from his friends and family. He would not talk with his girlfriend. Still, he could not see the problem. He says,

> I kept telling myself I feel fine, I know I'm thin, I want to gain weight, I do not have eating disorder thoughts. . . . All you ever hear about the disorder is that people

Eating Disorders Play No Favorites

Being successful, rich, or famous does not protect people from eating disorders. Some of the celebrities who have struggled with eating disorders include Mary-Kate Olsen of the Olsen twins, who was identified with anorexia at age eighteen, and Justine Bateman, who acted in television's *Family Ties* and developed bulimia. Victoria Beckham of the Spice Girls battled bulimia for years, as did *American Idol* winner Kelly Clarkson and former Spice Girl Geri Halliwell. Singers Janet Jackson and Elton John have both reported coping with eating disorders. Oprah Winfrey says that her eating disorder involves depending on food for comfort due to childhood abuse and she continues to struggle to lose her excess weight and eat healthily. People who have fought anorexia include singer and songwriter Fiona Apple, model Kate Dillon, and Miss America of 2008, Kirsten Haglund. *American Idol* judge Paula Abdul developed bulimia in high school. Today, she is a spokesperson for the National Eating Disorders Association (NEDA) and fights to persuade other eating disorder sufferers to seek help.

Mary-Kate Olsen of the Olsen twins is just one of many celebrities who have had an eating disorder.

who have them experience a distorted view of their body image, but this wasn't me. Now, while I was trying to fight this on my own, my body began to completely reject food. I could not keep down even a small meal. I was completely frightened of eating. I would eat and be in complete pain, I fought just to eat because I knew I needed to in order to get some type of nutrition to survive. I was in a battle with my own mind and body, and I was not equipped with the proper resources to fight it. It's really hard to explain and understand unless you've actually had an eating disorder.[45]

Finally in 2008, after almost four years of anorexia, Bergstrom knew he had to get help. His girlfriend cancelled their wedding and Bergstrom saw a doctor who told him his anorexia was killing him and that he had less than twelve months to live. Bergstrom turned to friends, family, treatment, and God. And at that point, he says he chose to fight the "ugly monster" of anorexia. He says, "I chose to live!"[46]

Anorexia Attacks a Little Child

Bergstrom used his intelligence and the support of others to confront his eating disorder. He was an adult and, at some level, could understand that he was in trouble, even though his anorexia did not follow the typical pattern of starving himself in order to lose weight. Elizabeth (not her real name) could not understand her anorexia because she was only five years old. Elizabeth's mother was constantly worrying about her own weight and always dieting. She talked so much about how she looked and what foods she ate that Elizabeth apparently imitated her mother. The little girl started to hate her body and restrict her food. Just like her mother, she began to pursue a perfect body. Soon, Elizabeth developed anorexia and suffered with it for years.

When she was fifteen years old, Elizabeth looked back on that sad time and remembered how bad she felt about herself. She says,

> I thought I was going to die and couldn't focus anymore. I was eating little pieces of paper to fill the void of food and running circles in my room every day to burn off the thoughts that filled my head. . . . I no longer have the perspective of a child, but now the perspective of a young adult. I know that perfect doesn't exist. Nobody is perfect; we all have our flaws and we can't possibly

Miss Florida Allison Kreiger believes stress and fear of failure caused her to become bulimic at age thirteen.

change them all. I know even when I have my good days and bad days that I cannot choose a life dictated by an eating disorder any longer.[47]

How Allison Found Bulimia

Choosing a life without an eating disorder is as difficult for people with bulimia as it is with anorexia, even though bulimia victims want desperately to change. Allison Kreiger fought this battle in high school. From the time she was five years old, says Allison, she was a "complete perfectionist." Her mother had been a champion baton twirler and Allison pressured herself to become a champion baton twirler, too. She wanted straight A's on her report card. She wanted to be the best at everything she did. The more pressure she put on herself, the more anxious and stressed she became. Allison believes that her stress and fear of failure began her road to bulimia at age thirteen. She recalls, "I remember vividly the day my eating disorder started. I had a bad day at the gym and was really upset. For some reason I got so worked up and it caused me to throw up. It just happened— something was triggered in my mind and it eventually led to a life consumed by an eating disorder and some very serious side effects." For more than three years, Allison binged and purged and sometimes fasted as well. She was able to keep her eating disorder a secret from everyone, but all that time she hated herself and wished she could stop. She thought constantly about food. She remembers, "My days were consumed by an illness I never expected, nor wanted, in my life."[48]

Lindsey's Bulimia Journey

Lindsey Hall knows about secrecy and being consumed. In the beginning of her nine-year battle with bulimia, she says, "I didn't want to tell anyone what I was doing, and I didn't want to stop." Besides, she thought, "I could stop anytime, probably tomorrow."[49] Since high school, Lindsey had been desperately unhappy about her weight. Classmates gave her the cruel nickname of "thunder thighs,"[50] even though she was no more than a few pounds overweight. She tried strict diets, but the dieting just made her binge because she was so hungry. Sometimes she would hide in her closet and eat spoonfuls of peanut butter directly from the jar. She took up cigarette smoking and gum chewing to kill her appetite, but they did not work. When she went away to college, she began sticking her finger down her throat to make herself vomit after a meal. By her sophomore year, she almost never ate in front of other people. She pretended she was on a diet and nibbled at meals. In private, however, she began to binge on larger and larger quantities of food. Sometimes she even shoplifted food to feed her habit. All she could think about was food and when she could indulge in her next binge. Vomiting got easy.

"I AM WAY TOO COOL A CHICK TO LET SOMETHING AS VILE AS AN EATING DISORDER NIP ME IN THE BUTT"

"My life for the past 5 years has been riddled with guilt, shame, anger, fear, bitterness, resentment, and anxiety. . . . I have been battling this for years, and I am done battling. I want to try living for a change." —Anonymous sufferer with anorexia and bulimia.

Anonymous, "I am way too cool a chick to let something as vile as an eating disorder nip me in the butt," Patients Speak, Personal Stories, F.E.A.S.T. (Families Empowered and Supporting Treatment of Eating Disorders). www.feast-ed.org/patient632.html.

Lindsey hated herself during her bingeing and purging. She believed she was ugly, a failure at life, and disgusting. When she married right after college graduation, she still kept her problem a secret. Her life revolved around shame and secrecy. She recalls,

> I became a meticulous housekeeper. . . . Sometimes I delayed throwing up while I vacuumed and washed dishes, eating all the time, to set the stage for the "cleaning" of my body.

> One thing I had to do between binges was run back to the store to restock the food. There were days when I had to rebake batches of brownies a couple of times. I

did dishes several times a day—I was averaging three to five binges everyday—and I was careful to check the toilet to be sure I'd left no traces. I hoarded bulk foods. I wanted everything to be orderly and clean in the closets and on bookshelves. THE ONLY THING THAT WAS NOT JUST PERFECT WAS ME![51]

A Mother's Experience

"It's a horrible, deceitful illness. As a parent you feel guilty and ashamed. When she was 14 and eating [chips], did we say, 'Be careful, you'll put on weight'? You start to blame yourself. People outside say, 'Just tell her to eat, get cross,' but crossness and anorexia don't go together." —Jo Kingsley, mother of a daughter with anorexia.

Quoted in Katy Guest, "Living with an Eating Disorder: A Mother, A Daughter and Anorexia," *Independent* (UK), April 1, 2007.

Bingeing Without Purging

Jean (full name withheld for her privacy) cannot keep her eating disorder a secret, although she does binge secretly. Her obesity is a telltale sign that she has a problem with food. It began when she was in high school, but Jean wonders if her dependence on food to soothe her anger, fears, and insecurity began even earlier. Jean's mother was anorexic. Jean says her mother's obsession with food led to her "stuffing her entire family while she starved herself." That was the beginning of Jean's disordered relationship with food. Then when Jean was eleven years old, her mother abandoned the family. Jean turned to food for comfort. Now in college, she starves herself on some days and binges on other days "by eating everything in the house."[52] Jean recognizes that she has a terrible problem and even has an idea about what caused it, but she cannot stop the monster from ruling her life. She says,

The truth is, I am scared to death. I have never had much control over my life, I've felt like a huge failure so many times. . . . I don't see this problem stopping. I have no control anymore and I don't know what to do. How can I take care of anything else in my life if all I can think of is food?? To me, overeating is about numbing myself, so I don't have to think or feel or know what's going on around me. About making myself so huge and unattractive and invisible no one will hurt me again but myself.[53]

Liz and Binge Eating

Jean's self-esteem is very low, and her self-image is poor. Self-hatred is a large part of Liz's binge eating disorder, too. Liz (full name withheld), at age twenty-nine, has been a binge eater since childhood. She is overweight but not obese. She describes herself as unhappy for no good reason (and is perhaps suffering from depression). Liz says, "I hate myself, I hate my job, and I hate my life."[54] When Liz was little, her parents fed her a very strict diet that included almost no sweets. Her mother strongly believed in "health foods." The only time Liz got candy or cookies was as a reward from neighbors when she did chores for them. Liz wonders if she is still rewarding herself by bingeing on sweets, but she thinks that she is punishing herself, too. She worries,

> I know that my binging [bingeing] is to do with being unhappy, but how do I pull myself out of it. I can't. . . . I . . . cook healthy and enjoy it, binge during the day on the sly, at night if my husband's out, read, play on the computer, listen to music, read, play my guitar, but it's like I'm filling in time waiting to live. Sometimes I feel I'm not living, I'm not alive, I'm dying, and I'm slowly killing myself by the crap I'm putting in my mouth. Please let it stop.[55]

Addicted to Binges

Many people with binge eating disorder say that they have an addiction to food, usually sweets or carbohydrates. Many experts agree—eating disorders are addictions. Binge eating disorder involves depression, anxiety, and using food as a medicine or drug to calm and numb painful emotions. Like any addict, the binge eater cannot control—or even think clearly about—what he or she eats.

Jennifer (full name withheld) describes a food addict's "recipe" for a binge:

> Start with the fried rice leftovers with intentions of eating like a normal, healthy individual. Sit down in front of the TV and don't bother paying attention to what you eat. Five minutes after finishing the fried rice discover the block of cheese that is going to waste. Get out the tortillas and start to make a quesadilla. While you wait for the microwave to heat it, eat as many slices of cheese as you can. While eating your first quesadilla, start your second. As that is heating up, finish the block of cheese. Now you are a bit thirsty and feel like you need something sweet, go ahead and pour yourself a bowl of cereal. Then a second and a third . . . until you have finished the box and are out of milk. Now start on the loaf of bread. Butter each slice, untoasted (toasting takes too long) and heap the cinnamon sugar on. Continue with each slice, one at a time until the loaf is gone. To get your mind off your severe stomach pain mix up the brownies. Use a spoon to eat the mixture raw. Wash this down with 2–3 cans of diet root beer. Now go into your bedroom, change into your jammies, pull the covers up over your head, and try to fall asleep.[56]

Bingeing Away the Pain

Sometimes, bingeing begins early in life as a way of dealing with an abusive situation. Ron Saxen began turning to food for comfort when he was just a boy. His parents were strict disciplinarians. His mother would keep a written list of everything he had done wrong during the day. After he had gone to bed, his father would come home, read the list, and then decide whether to wake him up and punish him. Many nights, Saxen could not sleep for fear of his father. He would lie in bed—sweating and

Binge eaters are like any other addicts in that they cannot control their urges.

waiting. The boy learned to deal with his fear with candy. He kept chocolate bars hidden in his closet. When his anxiety got too bad, he would get up, grab a bar, and take it back to eat in bed. He remembers, "And when I ate it, it felt good. I forgot about what was about to happen, and then I went back and did it again and again and again."[57] When he grew up, Saxen continued to calm himself with food. Whenever he was unhappy or worried, he binged on fast food and candy. He could eat as many as fifteen thousand calories at one time.

To Fight the Secret Monster

Often, people with binge eating disorder are too ashamed to tell anyone what is happening to them. Like people with bulimia, they try to get over the addiction themselves. They try to use willpower alone to conquer their need to binge. Usually, however, no one with bulimia or binge eating disorder can recover and heal without professional help. The same is true for people with anorexia, who may not even realize that they are addicted to starvation. Eating disorders are real diseases that require real treatment and sometimes years of hard work to overcome.

THE DIAGNOSIS AND TREATMENT OF EATING DISORDERS

E xperts disagree about the most effective way to treat eating disorders. They are not even sure if today's standards of diagnosis are accurate and useful. Not everyone with an eating disorder fits into a neat diagnostic category. Most eating disorder professionals, however, are convinced that diagnosis, treatment, and therapy are absolutely necessary for anyone with an eating disorder. Professionals have strong evidence that the earlier an eating disorder is diagnosed and treated, the better the chance is for recovery.

Diagnosing Eating Disorders

Before treatment can begin, the eating disorder must be diagnosed correctly. In the United States, eating disorders are diagnosed by medical doctors and psychiatrists, using the *Diagnostic and Statistical Manual of Mental Disorders, Text Revision (DSM-IV-TR)*. This manual from the American Psychiatric Association contains the criteria for identifying a wide variety of disorders of thoughts, feelings, and behaviors. Currently, *DSM-IV-TR* is generally agreed to be the best tool available for recognizing and labeling mental and emotional problems. *DSM-IV-TR* defines eating disorders as a range or spectrum of conditions that involve both "severe disturbances in eating behavior" and "distress or excessive concern about body shape or weight."[58] *DSM-IV-TR* recognizes three major classifications of eating disorders: anorexia nervosa, bulimia nervosa, and a catchall classification named eating disorders not otherwise specified (EDNOS).

A Diagnosis of Anorexia

The criteria for a diagnosis of anorexia nervosa include four major symptoms. First, the patient's body weight is less than 85 percent of the minimally acceptable weight for the patient's height and age. This low weight cannot be due to a physical illness; *DSM-IV-TR* states that it must be caused by the person's refusal to eat enough to maintain a good body weight. The patient must also show a fear of weight gain or anxiety about getting fat, even if he or she is underweight or emaciated. Body image is distorted, and the patient believes he or she is fat or believes that his or her self-worth is measured by body shape or insists that he or she is healthy and normal. Finally, if the patient is a girl or woman, she must have missed at least three menstrual periods in a row.

Clinical professionals who diagnose anorexia conduct interviews with the patient and family, perform medical examinations, and administer psychological tests.

Since some people with anorexia may sometimes purge, anorexia nervosa is divided into two types. In the "restricting type," the patient simply starves him- or herself. In the "purging type,"[59] the patient may alternate fasting with occasional bingeing that is followed by any kind of purging, such as vomiting or using enemas, laxatives, or diuretics.

Clinicians (professionals who treat and diagnose patients) make a diagnosis of anorexia nervosa by conducting a medical examination, interviewing the patient and family members, and by administering psychological tests that ask about eating behaviors and self-image. One such test is called the Body Shape Questionnaire. Patients answer questions such as whether they think it is unfair that other people are thinner, whether they have cried over their body shape, and whether eating even a small meal makes them feel fat. The test includes thirty-four questions about feelings, food, and body image. Patients answer each question by marking it in a range from 1 (Never) to 6 (Always). The clinician scores the test by adding up the numbers for all the questions. Higher scores indicate poorer body image and greater concerns about body shape. With test results such as these and a professional evaluation of the patient, the clinician diagnoses anorexia only if the patient meets all the criteria listed in *DSM-IV-TR*.

A Diagnosis of Bulimia

Bulimia nervosa is diagnosed similarly, in that the patient must evidence a poor body image and test as significantly worried about body weight and shape. The Body Shape Questionnaire may be used to measure self-image and anxiety about weight. The criteria for diagnosing bulimia include definitions for both bingeing and purging. Binges are defined as repeated episodes of eating "an amount of food that is definitely larger than most people would eat during a similar period of time and under similar circumstances."[60] The patient must feel out of control and unable to stop the binge. Purges must repeatedly follow binges and can include vomiting, using laxatives, diuretics, and/or enemas, and excessive exercise. For a diagnosis of bulimia nervosa, the binges and purges must have occurred at least twice a week for three months.

"Not Otherwise Specified"

Eating disorder not otherwise specified (EDNOS) is the diagnosis for anyone who is eating disordered but does not fit the diagnostic category of anorexia nervosa or bulimia nervosa. Binge eating disorder is classified as an EDNOS because it is an eating disorder with bingeing and poor body image but missing the purging of bulimia. Currently, *DSM-IV-TR* labels binge eating disorder as a category needing further study to determine if it should be included as a separate diagnosis in the future.

An eating disorder not otherwise specified (EDNOS) is defined as any eating disorder other than anorexia nervosa or bulimia nervosa.

EDNOS is also the diagnosis for a female with all the anorexic symptoms except that she still has her period. It is the diagnosis for a bulimic patient who has not binged and purged as often as twice a week for three months. EDNOS is used for people who have symptoms not listed in *DSM-IV-TR*, too. It includes those who chew on food and then spit it out instead of swallowing it. It can be used for a patient who purges after eating small portions of "forbidden" foods, such as one who eats one cookie and then vomits it up.

The Problems with *DSM-IV-TR*

Many clinicians are extremely dissatisfied with the EDNOS diagnosis. They also believe that all eating disorder criteria are too strict and rigid. For example, in 2008 researchers at Brown University and Rhode Island Hospital complained that more than 90 percent of the patients they saw were diagnosed with either EDNOS or binge eating disorder. Lead researcher Mark Zimmerman said, "The NOS [not otherwise specified] category of the *DSM-IV* was intended to be . . . a diagnostic option for relatively infrequent cases. This study has shown that [EDNOS] cases predominate and suggests a problem . . . with this class of disorders."[61] Zimmerman says the research proves that the criteria should be loosened and that binge eating disorder must be included as a separate diagnosis.

Clinicians want to identify eating disorders in the early stages because that is when treatment works best. In the early stages, however, a fasting girl may not have lost quite enough body fat that her period stops, even though she is obviously anorexic and in great danger. Clinicians know such a patient has anorexia, but they cannot diagnose her according to *DSM-IV-TR* criteria except with EDNOS. At other times, a patient may have anorexia with symptoms of bulimia or a bulimic patient may purge only once a week. A diagnosis of EDNOS is required but it does little to describe the patient's obvious eating disorder. Clinicians worry that the vague EDNOS diagnosis could delay or discourage treatment. "Practically speaking," points out the eating disorder Web site Something Fishy, these people "are suffering with an Eating Disorder. [They are] in danger of potentially deadly physical complications and . . . need to make a choice for recovery."[62]

From Diagnosis to Treatment

Making a "choice for recovery" means wanting to overcome the eating disorder, no matter what the diagnosis. It means choosing treatment and therapy. Yet even with treatment, the longer an eating disorder lasts, the harder it is to overcome. According to the Cleveland Clinic's Disease Management Project, about one-third of patients recover completely, one-third greatly improve but still have some symptoms, and one-third continue to have an eating disorder.

Whatever the eating disorder diagnosis, recovery is most likely with early treatment and intervention. Ideally it involves a team approach that includes medical intervention, nutritional help, and psychotherapy (talk therapy with a psychologist or other therapist). Sometimes medications and family therapy are needed, too. The kind of intervention required depends on the severity of the eating disorder, the immediate medical dangers, and the patient's motivation to change. Psychiatrist B. Timothy Walsh explains:

Several important goals to achieve, in order of decreasing urgency include:

- Correct potentially life-threatening health complications (e.g., heart irregularities, low blood pressure, dehydration).

- Minimize risks of self-harm, such as suicidal behavior.

- Restore weight to normal.

- Develop normal eating behavior and eliminate binge eating and purging.

- Address psychological and psychosocial issues (e.g., low self-esteem, body image distortion, problems in interpersonal relationships [relating to other people and getting along with them]).

- Maintain long-term recovery.[63]

First: Save the Life

The top priority for treatment in patients with eating disorders is always medical treatment. This means immediate hospitaliza-

A Day in the Life

Eating disorders physician David B. Herzog and his colleagues describe an example of the typical, very structured days in residential treatment that helps people recover. (This structure would include academic classes later, when the patient is ready.)

8:00 A.M. Community Meeting

8:30 A.M. Breakfast/relaxation session

9:30 A.M. Assertiveness training [learning to speak one's mind and stand up for oneself]

10:30 A.M. Snack/relaxation session

10:45 A.M. One-to-one talk with member of the nursing staff

11:15 A.M. [Group discussion about how to cope with changes in one's life]

12:00 Lunch followed by relaxation session

1:00 P.M. Educational video (documentary on body image) followed by group discussion

2:00 P.M. One-to-one meeting with psychotherapist.

3:00 P.M. Snack/relaxation session

3:30 P.M. Group discussion of how to structure free time

4:30 P.M. One-to-one talk with member of nursing staff

5:00 P.M. Dinner/relaxation session

6:00 P.M. [Group meeting]

7:00 P.M. Reading/journal writing/receiving visitors/talking with other patients

8:00 P.M. Snack/relaxation session

David B. Herzog, Debra L. Franko, and Pat Cable, *Unlocking the Mysteries of Eating Disorders: A Life-Saving Guide to Your Child's Treatment and Recovery.* New York: McGraw-Hill, 2007, pp. 74–75.

tion for patients whose body weight has dropped to 75 percent of the minimum normal for their height and age or who have other dangerous medical issues. The effects of malnutrition or bingeing and purging may be treated by intravenous fluid replacement. Medications may be administered for blood pressure and heart problems. Eating disorder physician David B. Herzog and his colleagues add,

For those who don't eat adequately on their own, naso-gastric feeding is sometimes necessary. A slender tube is inserted through the individual's nose into [the] stomach, a process that feels strange or mildly uncomfortable but is not painful and does not involve surgery. Once the tube is in place, liquid feedings are introduced and carefully monitored to give [the] body the sustenance it so urgently needs.[64]

Because they are forced to eat healthy meals in the hospital, some people resist medical treatment. One worried mother, for example, remembers watching her teenaged anorexic son lying in his hospital bed "and trying to tear the IV out of his arm."[65] The first time that Courtney (not her real name) was forced by her mother to see her doctor for her bulimia, the teen was furious. Her mother reports, "On the way to his office, she urged me to turn the car around, claiming that she felt fine and that my worries about her health were 'ridiculous.' . . . At one point, my daughter was madder at me than I'd ever seen her. . . . She was so riled up that I was afraid she'd open the car door and dash out."[66] Eating disorder medical specialist Ira M. Sacker recalls meeting a young anorexic girl just admitted to the hospital. The girl was screaming, fighting, and pulling her mother's hair. When Sacker had persuaded the teenager to calm down and told her she needed to be hospitalized, she "laughed and refused—totally, absolutely, adamantly."[67]

Fortunately, explains Herzog, most people, no matter how much they resist at first, accept the need to be hospitalized within a few days. As they calm down and begin to feel better, they are able to cooperate with medical treatment. Then, once an eating disordered patient is medically stable, he or she can be released from the hospital, and the real treatment and intervention can begin.

Residential Treatment and Therapy

For many people, treatment works best in a residential or inpatient setting. This can entail living at a treatment center for a period that may last from perhaps thirty days to as long as a year. Bergstrom, for example, chose a residential institution called Canopy Cove when he needed to get help for his eating disorder. In this treatment center, he was removed from all the stresses and responsibilities in his life that were maintaining his anorexia. While he was a patient he explained,

> I am in treatment all day, going through therapy and re-training myself to eat properly again. . . . I have learned a lot in the first few weeks, but the process for my recovery is an ongoing, uphill battle. Canopy Cove allows you to step out of your normal comfort zone, challenging you to be free to experience new things. They use various methods of treatment to remedy the mind, body and spirit. These

Many people with eating disorders have found that residential or inpatient treatment is highly effective in overcoming their disorder.

therapy techniques include music, art, yoga, and body image therapy and allow clients to enjoy the simplicities of life. I am beginning to understand my disorder and am starting to separate myself from it. The overall goal of recovery is to completely separate your mind and body from the disorder, giving individuals full control of their life.[68]

A part of Bergstrom's treatment was nutritional. The center provided the healthy balanced meals that his body needed. Part of the process was talk therapy in which he faced his emotions, insecurities, and fear of failure. Part of his treatment was educational. Bergstrom learned healthy ways to handle his stress and how to continue his recovery after he left the residential center. It was a long process, but he did recover and today is an eating disorder activist, speaker, and writer.

Learning to Eat and to Live

Residential centers can be the best treatment options for young people, too. May (not her real name) entered a residential center when she was sixteen years old and was diagnosed with both anorexia and bulimia. She remembers,

> I didn't want to go to any institution. . . . But the residential center I went to looked more like a comfy house than a hospital—that part I liked. I felt that everything I did there was under a microscope and monitored by staff—that part I didn't like. My days were organized around group meetings [where the patients could help and support each other], meetings with therapists, academic classes, and meals. Art therapy was part of the program as well.[69]

At first, May found the regimen very difficult. She says,

> I felt torn apart about doing what I'd vowed I'd never, ever do—gain weight. And there was no doubt in my mind that I was the fattest patient there and that if I started to eat, I'd never be able to stop. . . . After eating, I'd feel that parts of me were inflating like a balloon, and that was upsetting—at times, almost more than I could

handle. Sometimes I wanted to vomit, and I knew some tricks to use . . . but I didn't think I could succeed without getting caught.[70]

Eventually May was able to share her fears with the nurses and therapists at the center. May says that they helped her develop a "game plan"[71] to deal with her bad feelings. As May got healthier, the day came that she began to believe she could get well. She began to trust in herself and her treatment and to feel hope for the future.

RECOVERED AND GRATEFUL

"To all the parents reading this, who are struggling to find their sons and daughters trapped in a body overtaken by an eating disorder . . . KEEP GOING. Your child may not be able to tell you right now, they may not even realize it, but they appreciate what you are doing more than you can know." —Anonymous patient now recovered.

Anonymous, "It Was Almost a Year Before I Let Her Touch Me or Hug Me," Patients Speak: Personal Stories: Letters, F.E.A.S.T. (Families Empowered and Supporting Treatment of Eating Disorders), May 2009. www.feast-ed.org/patient623.html.

The Maudsley Treatment Method

Not everyone needs residential treatment for an eating disorder. Many people receive outpatient treatment. Some people "graduate" from a residential center to outpatient treatment. Outpatients may have several appointments a week with therapists, nutritionists, and medical doctors, but they remain at home during treatment. For teens, family involvement often plays a critical role in this treatment.

The best-studied and most promising approach is called the Maudsley method, because it was developed at the Maudsley Hospital in London, England. With the Maudsley method, parents play a major role in fighting the eating disorders. The parents are taught three phases of treatment behaviors. In the first phase, the parent is responsible for restoring proper meals and nutrition. Health, not gaining weight, is emphasized. The par-

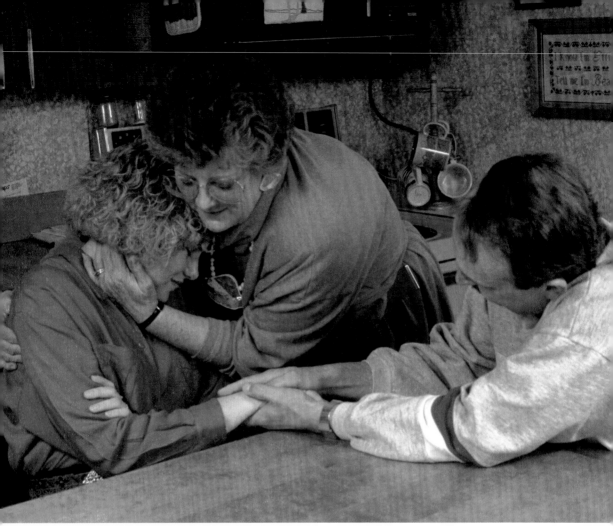

The Maudsley treatment method has parents playing a major role in helping their child fight his or her eating disorder.

ent must prepare, serve, and monitor all the teen's meals and snacks. One mother used this method with her son Greg (not his real name) who had anorexia. The mother's Maudsley therapist told her to "think of anorexia as a loud voice in Greg's mind that instructed him to lose weight and restrict his eating. The idea was to lower the volume of anorexia's message, which was now blasting, and to amplify the voice of health." When Greg's mother served him his plate at mealtime, she might say something like, "I know this looks like a lot to you and that you are feeling bad about eating it. Try to have faith in what your doctors, Dad, and I are telling you—eating what we ask will help you get better."[72]

After the teen is doing well with eating his or her meals, parents advance to the second phase of Maudsley treatment. They must now help the teen to prepare and/or choose his or her own meals and snacks. The parent still guides and monitors, but the teen has more independence and is trusted to try to eat normally. Once this phase is completed successfully, the family moves on to phase three. They can begin to work on the feelings and problems in the teen's life that may have triggered the eating disorder. Parents have professional help throughout the phases of the Maudsley method. The eating-disordered teen is usually monitored weekly by a medical doctor and educated about the medical dangers of his or her eating disorder. In addition, the teen sees a nutritionist regularly to learn about food and health. A family therapist provides weekly counseling for everyone in the family.

MISSION ACCOMPLISHED

"My goal in recovery, because of my thoughts on Eating Disorders, was to build my self-esteem . . . to learn to love myself completely and be comfortable being me." —Amy Medina, recovered anorexic and founder of the Web site Something Fishy.

Amy Medina, "The Other Side," Something Fishy, May 2000. www.something-fishy .org/reach/otherside_amy.php.

The Maudsley method has proved helpful for teens with anorexia, bulimia, and some kinds of EDNOS, especially when the eating disorder is caught early. A 2008 study showed that after Maudsley treatment within the first three years of onset, 60 to 90 percent of young people were still fully recovered after five years.

What Works with Binge Eating Disorder?

A few studies suggest that Maudsley-based family therapy can be successful for people with binge eating disorder, too, but such treatments are just beginning to be used. Little is known about its overall effectiveness with binge eating, though. As a matter of fact, the diagnosis of binge eating is so new that no one knows what treatments might be most effective. Sacker believes talk therapy is best. He says that people must explore the underlying emotional issues and traumas that trigger eating disorders in susceptible brains. Sacker explains, "Trauma comes in many forms and doesn't have to be related to abuse or horrifying experiences. Trauma can be the death of a loved

Eating disorders specialist Ira Sacker believes that talk therapy (shown here) for binge eaters is an effective means of treatment.

one, moving away from home, or changing employment; sometimes it's the sense of being lost that comes from having no real identity."[73]

Sacker helps people with eating disorders explore their possibilities. He encourages them to talk about what they love to do, think about how they want to live their lives, and learn what makes them special. He also uses talk therapy to help people deal with trauma in a healthier way than with food. Katherine (real name withheld) was a teen with binge eating disorder. She was working with Sacker and doing well. As she talked over her emotional problems, her eating disorder was improving. She was losing weight and developing self-confidence. Then Katherine suddenly relapsed, and her binge eating returned. Sacker discovered that her family was expecting a visit from Katherine's grandparents. Finally Katherine told Sacker a terrible secret—her grandfather had sexually abused her when she was five years old. With Katherine's permission, Sacker discussed the situation with Katherine's mother, who canceled the expected visit. Sacker reports, "Katherine's collapse didn't stop once she revealed her history of sexual abuse. Over the next couple of weeks, however, her emotions stabilized and we started moving forward again."[74]

Cognitive Behavioral Therapy

Katherine's supportive family and therapy helped her to deal with her trauma. Other people with eating disorders may need different kinds of talk therapy. Cognitive behavioral therapy (CBT) is the method chosen by many eating disorder experts. Rather than talking about trauma, CBT emphasizes learning a different, healthy way of thinking and behaving. Typically, the CBT therapist may ask the patient to keep a daily log of everything he or she eats and to write down the thoughts or feelings that came with the meal. Then, together, patient and therapist discuss this record and explore how disordered behaviors could be changed. They talk about healthy ways to deal with stress. They may also explore mistaken beliefs, such as an anorexic person's conviction that he or she is too fat. The goal is to reduce and eventually eliminate starving, bingeing,

Relapses

During treatment for an eating disorder, relapses are common. A relapse is a return to disordered eating patterns after a period of improvement. Relapses seem to happen to about 60 percent of people during their recovery process. They are most common within the first six months of treatment. People who have been symptom free for a year are often safe from relapsing. Relapses can be frightening and make a patient feel like a failure, but clinicians say that relapsing is not a sign that treatment is not working. It is just one step on the road to complete recovery. As treatment continues, the chance of relapse becomes less and less.

or purging behavior. Some of the ways that CBT approaches eating behavior include drawing pictures of healthy bodies, learning facts about appropriate calorie intake, substituting binges with pleasant activities such as listening to music, talking about what makes people successes or failures, and studying the medical effects of disordered eating patterns. Even when the person cooperates and wants to change, however, the process can take a long time. Herzog explains, "For some patients, treatment can take years."[75]

Medications for Eating Disorders

Because of long-term problems with depression and anxiety, many doctors prescribe medication as a part of eating disorder treatment. Mood-altering drugs for depression and anxiety can help some anorexic adults, but so far, research suggests that the improvement is slight. With bulimia, however, tests with adults suggest that binge eating and vomiting may be 75 percent reduced with antidepressant medicine, perhaps because these drugs change the levels of serotonin in the brain. Some doctors believe antidepressants help teens as well. A few drugs have also been tried on adults with binge eating disorder. So far, most drugs that have been tried for adults have not been tested with teens. Many doctors prescribe mood-altering drugs for eating-disordered teens only if they suffer with depression or suicidal thoughts or are in danger of injuring themselves. Other doctors will prescribe them to see if the teen's mood will improve. However, Herzog points out that "there are no magic bullets; that is, no drug has proven consistently effective in the treatment of these disorders."[76]

It Takes Dedication to Succeed

No matter what the therapy or drug, treatment for eating disorders is never straightforward or simple. Yet, most people do find the courage to travel the long road toward recovery.

Tackling the Larger Issue: Prevention of Eating Disorders

People suffer when they develop an eating disorder, and recovery can be a complicated ordeal. Eating disorder experts, therefore, are searching for ways to prevent eating disorders before they start. Walsh says, "It is critically important that the search continue for more precise and useful definitions of eating disorders and for improved methods to treat them. An even more desirable goal would be to mount an effective effort to prevent their occurrence in the first place by targeting young children and adolescents [teens] who may be most at risk for these illnesses."[77] Prevention of eating disorders might be accomplished by identifying and treating individuals at risk. This is called "targeted" prevention because it is aimed at the people who are most likely to develop eating disorders. "Universal"[78] prevention is another way to tackle the problem. It involves educating society at large and attempting to change beliefs and attitudes about body image and self-worth in whole groups of people.

Diagnosis for Early Intervention

If medical professionals could identify people who are likely to develop an eating disorder in response to stress, they could stop the problem before it begins. One way to do this would be to know the genetics of eating disorder vulnerability. NIMH has funded an ongoing genetic study of anorexia that began in 2005. Ten research facilities around the United States are collecting genetic samples from four hundred families that have at least two members with anorexia. At the same time that these people are receiving treatment, they also give blood samples and medical histories to the researchers. Researchers will compare the samples and look for specific genetic differences in family members who have anorexia.

One of these researchers is Maria LaVia at the University of Pittsburgh's Western Psychiatric Institute and Clinic. She believes that genetic studies will someday make it possible to identify the specific genes or areas of multiple genes that cause a vul-

Some researchers believe genetic studies will someday identify specific genes or multiple genes that cause a susceptibility to anorexia.

nerability to anorexia. With this knowledge, it will be possible for doctors to diagnose anorexia with a genetic test. LaVia says it will be as easy as diagnosing an infection by identifying the virus in the medical laboratory. This is important because medical doctors would be able to diagnose the anorexia even when the disorder is in its earliest stages. They would not have to worry about anorexic behavioral criteria or EDNOS. They would know, for sure, that treatment was needed. Such knowledge might also help people to seek treatment earlier in the course of the eating disorder. LaVia explains, "Patients often blame themselves because they've caused this illness themselves by not eating or by eating and throwing up."[79] She believes patients and their families often resist seeking help because they are ashamed. She hopes for a future in which no one feels at fault about an eating disorder. She works toward a time when long-term anorexia is prevented by simple, genetic diagnosis that leads to immediate treatment and early recovery.

A BRIGHTER FUTURE AHEAD

"The field of eating disorders (prevention, treatment, and research) is dynamic; it is always changing and growing in new and positive directions. Although knowledge has increased substantially over the last several decades, there is still a great deal to learn." —David B. Herzog, Debra L. Franko, and Pat Cable

David B. Herzog, Debra L. Franko, and Pat Cable, *Unlocking the Mysteries of Eating Disorders*. New York: McGraw-Hill, 2007, p. 243.

A similar study of the genetics of binge eating disorder began in 2008 in Toronto, Canada, at the Centre for Addiction and Mental Health. Researchers want to understand how genes might put people at risk and how the gene variations might interact with the environment to cause people to develop a kind of addiction to certain types of foods. In the future, if scientists could identify genetic risk, they might even be able to develop specific drugs that could dampen the effects of the genes and prevent binge eating disorder from beginning.

Science's Search for Risk Factors

Research into the genetic causes of eating disorders holds promise for the future, but it will be a long time before the results lead to prevention. Other researchers concentrate on the psychological or environmental factors that may trigger the genetic predisposition. These researchers look for specific interventions that might protect vulnerable people and give them the ability to avoid disordered eating patterns. First, the risk factors for eating disorders need to be scientifically identified, so that researchers know which people to target for intervention.

Identification of risk factors was the goal of psychologist Aitziber Pascual Jimeno at the University of the Basque Country in Spain in 2008. She studied 433 young women who either already had an eating disorder or had been diagnosed as at risk for one. She drew up an "emotional profile" of each woman. The profile included a measure of each woman's feelings about her body shape, tests of self-esteem and anxiety levels, and questions about attitudes concerning dieting and weight. Jimeno also measured what each woman did when she was feeling negative about herself or feeling anxious and stressed. She wanted to know if the women talked about their bad, sad, worried emotions to others instead of holding their feelings inside. Jimeno discovered that she could use some psychological factors as measures of risk. She found that the three risk factors that "alert to greater risk of developing an eating disorder are when the emotional state of the person is excessively influenced by diet, weight and body shape, when self-esteem is low, and when, in anxiety situations, emotions are not expressed."[80]

Targeted Risk Prevention

Can risk factors be lowered if professionals target vulnerable people with prevention programs? Could eating disorders be prevented before they even begin? This was the question asked by psychologist Eric Stice and his research team. They concentrated on one risk factor, which they called "body dissatisfaction."[81] They wanted to test the value of targeted prevention programs for young women with high body dissatisfaction because

Targeted risk prevention therapy concentrates on "body dissatisfaction" in young women between the ages of thirteen to twenty-nine.

they believed that this emotion could lead to eating disorders. The researchers studied 481 young women between the ages of thirteen and twenty-nine who were dissatisfied with their body shape and weight.

The women were divided into four groups and for one month in 2005, each group was in a different kind of program.

One group was given psychological tests but not helped in any other way. Another group was directed to write about their feelings about weight, self-esteem, and body image. The third group was enrolled in a healthy weight class. These women learned about how to eat less fats and sugars and to increase their exercise. They also kept food and exercise diaries. The last group participated in a "thin-ideal" intervention. They discussed and criticized attitudes about having to be thin to be worthwhile. They did role-playing exercises in which they had to talk someone out of "pursuing the thin ideal"[82] and explain why it was wrong.

In 2008, three years after the intervention programs, the researchers checked on how the women were doing. Some of

Appropriate Treatment for All

Currently, many people with eating disorders must do without or struggle to access appropriate treatment, even though they want to recover. Long-term therapy and residential treatment are very expensive. While insurance companies may pay for treatment of serious psychiatric illnesses, some insurance companies justify their refusal to pay for eating disorders treatment by classifying these illnesses as emotional rather than psychiatric problems. The Academy for Eating Disorders issued a position statement in 2009 that strongly opposes such classifications. The authors say, in part, that eating disorders are "biologically based" and that

> science affirms with a reasonable degree of medical and scientific

certainty that eating disorders are significantly heritable [genetically determined]; influenced by alterations of brain function; significantly impair cognitive function, judgment, and emotional stability; and restrict the life activities of persons afflicted with these illnesses. Accordingly, the denial or restriction of equitable [fair] and sufficient treatment necessary to avert serious health consequences and risk of death is untenable [indefensible] and should be vigorously protested.

Kelly L. Klump, Cynthia M. Bulik, Walter H. Kaye, Janet Treasure, and Edward Tyson, "Academy for Eating Disorders Position Paper: Eating Disorders Are Serious Mental Illnesses," Academy for Eating Disorders. www .aedweb.org/policy/AED_MentalIllness.pdf.

them did develop eating disorders. But those who learned about healthy weight or learned to question the thin ideal did better, with about 60 percent fewer cases of eating disorders than the other two groups. In addition, the group that got healthy weight information had 55 percent fewer cases of obesity (which can be related to binge eating disorder). The researchers had strong evidence that educational programs can prevent cases of eating disorders. They decided to use this evidence to develop an eating disorder prevention program that could be used in the real world.

The Body Project

At the Oregon Research Institute, Stice and his research team developed the Body Project. It is a prevention program designed to reduce the risk of eating disorders in young people. Based on their studies, the researchers have incorporated healthy weight education and education about the "thin ideal" that causes low self-esteem and poor body image. The project is being used in high schools and colleges around the country, both to attack eating disorders and the problem of obesity. It can be targeted at people at risk or who feel at risk because they feel bad about their bodies and weight. However, it may also be used universally. Stice and his colleagues train high school and college teachers and counselors to lead the project in their schools. Body Project education includes learning about social attitudes that associate happiness with being thin. It involves role playing and criticizing the thin ideal. It includes learning to like one's body the way it is and then learning to eat healthily and exercise. It discourages diets.

After the educational part of the program is complete, participants engage in "body activism." They have to come up with "small nonviolent acts" that fight the idea that body size and shape determine self-worth. For example, Kelsey Hertel, a high school student in Oregon, completed the Body Project program when she was a junior. Then, she and a friend made signs that read, "YOU ARE BEAUTIFUL. DON'T BE SOMEONE THAT YOU'RE NOT. BE YOURSELF." The girls posted their signs in all the girls' bathrooms in their school. Kelsey believes that her ac-

The Body Project encourages girls to learn to like their bodies by incorporating healthy weight education and criticizing the "thin ideal."

tivism helps counteract poor self-image in fellow students who see the posters. She says, "They'd see the signs and say things like, 'That's encouraging because I always feel so fat and gross and ugly.'"[83]

The Power of Society's Message

Kelsey has learned not to be influenced by social attitudes about weight and body image. Her healthy view of herself may protect her and her friends from becoming depressed and stressed about their bodies and weight. Many experts and researchers believe that social beliefs and attitudes, especially those presented in the media, play a big part in the development of eating disorders. Beautiful, super-thin models appear in fashion magazines. Television and movie stars are often thin to the point of emaciation. Athletes who seem to be without an ounce of body fat are admired as ideal. Crash diets guaranteed to make people beautiful pop up as ads on the Internet. Little children play with fashion dolls with impossibly perfect bodies.

Everywhere that young people turn, they find the message that people have to be skinny to be good looking, worthwhile, and successful. Parents and friends often contribute to these messages. They may say critical things about overweight people. They may constantly talk about their own diets and complain about their bodies. They may bully people who look different. Even school coaches may push student athletes to lose weight or exercise more. All of these social messages can contribute to worry about body shape, unhealthy dieting, and eventually perhaps rejecting food and starving, throwing up to avoid gaining weight, or bingeing from hunger and depression.

Attacking Social Messages

Scientists and educators in several universities are trying to use Body Project education to help all young people feel better about their bodies and to avoid disordered eating. They want to fight the social and cultural messages and say that people are OK even if they are not thin at all, much less unnaturally thin. This is the universal approach to preventing eating disorders. It is information offered to everyone to help them resist the social attitudes that make them dislike their bodies. The hope is that such programs will also reduce the cases of eating disorders.

The national college sorority Tri Delta has begun a prevention program called Reflections, based on the Body Project. Every new member of the sorority attends the program during orientation. Reflections was developed by psychologist Carolyn Becker. According to the Reflections Web site, "the program does not focus on eating disorders; rather, it emphasizes creating and reaffirming positive and healthy personal body image through a variety of structured discussions, activities, and exercises."[84] Some of these discussions are about healthy eating and exercise, some teach critical thinking about media messages, and some address body image and self-esteem. Participants are encouraged to spread the healthy messages when they talk with others. They are asked to stand up against the idea that people have to be physically perfect to be worthwhile. Sorority members also try to raise "national awareness" of the problem of eating disorders. Every year, Tri Delta runs a campaign called

Danger on the Web

Something Fishy is a Web site dedicated to recovery, but it warns that not all eating disorder sites share the same goal. So-called "pro-ana" and "pro-mia" Web sites encourage people to continue anorexic and bulimic behaviors. Something Fishy states,

> Visiting websites that encourage Anorexia or Bulimia as a "lifestyle" is another signal that someone may be suffering with an Eating Disorder (think of an alcoholic who continuously hangs around with other drinkers, or a drug addict who keeps company with other addicts). It is an indication that the sufferer may be in denial, or may be looking to justify to themselves and those around them that their behaviors are okay, are safe, are "normal." While it can

be comforting to a sufferer to be amongst those who understand, it is not safe or healthy for them to be in an environment where the behaviors of an Eating Disorder are encouraged or justified as okay, safe, fine or "just a way to lose weight"—they are not. They are dangerous, self-defeating, self-destructive, and very often, life threatening.

Professional organizations such as the National Association of Anorexia Nervosa and Associate Disorders fight to remove these sites from the World Wide Web. The goal for the future is an Internet experience that promotes recovery only.

Something Fishy.org., "This Is a PRO-Recovery Website," press release. www.something-fishy.org/sfwed/prorecovery.php.

"Fat Free Talk Week." Members sign pledges and promise not to "fat talk" for five days. They do not complain about their own bodies or mention diets or listen to anyone else talk about being fat. They say only positive things about their bodies and the bodies of their friends. Tri Delta says, "Friends don't let friends Fat Talk."[85]

Are Anti-Obesity Campaigns Harmful Social Messages?

Talk about fat is not limited to young women and girls. Scientists, doctors, politicians, and educators today say that the United States is suffering an obesity epidemic. They worry that excessive weight and obesity are a public health problem among young people that must be addressed. Young people are bombarded with messages about avoiding obesity and reducing calorie intake. Many are being encouraged to go on a diet. Some eating disorder experts are deeply concerned that this constant warning about being overweight is causing an increase in eating disorders among vulnerable teens. Some may go on a diet that triggers anorexia. Others may be so determined to lose weight that they develop bulimia. Some may feel so discouraged and hate their overweight bodies so much that they binge for comfort and become obese. Social work expert Frances M. Berg warns, for example, "An awareness is needed . . . that overemphasis on the risks of overweight can quickly escalate for vulnerable children into promoting thin mania, disturbed eating, and social discrimination [e.g., being bullied by classmates for being fat]."[86]

Walsh says the issue of anti-obesity campaigns causing eating disorders is a "hot button topic . . . among eating disorder specialists and obesity experts." Walsh agrees that obesity is a serious problem that can lead to health complications. "However," he explains, "some clinicians and researchers have been concerned that encouraging dieting may increase the risk of eating disorders, particularly among adolescent females, and that weight loss programs might do more harm than good."[87] In one study, researchers put a group of obese adults on a very low-calorie diet, designed to produce quick weight loss at the beginning of the treatment. When that part of the diet ended and people were allowed to eat more normally again, 30 percent of them started to have binge-eating episodes. They had not been binge eaters before the treatment started.

KNOWLEDGE IS POWER

"Eating disorder educational programs can alert parents and children to the nature of eating disorders, the risks involved in acting out an eating disorder, how to recognize when they or someone they know needs help, and most importantly, how to get help."—Joanna Poppink

Joanna Poppink, "Eating Disorder Education: Benefits for Parents and Teens," Something Fishy.org: Articles by Professionals. www.something-fishy.org/doctors/doc_article004.php.

Balanced Messages to Prevent Eating Disorders

Of course, most people who go on a diet do not develop an eating disorder. However, since campaigns to reduce overweight and extreme dieting can backfire in people with a predisposition for an eating disorder, many experts suggest that dieting should be discouraged. Several studies have found strong evidence that anorexia and bulimia can be triggered by beginning a diet, too. Walsh suggests,

> Perhaps, as in many areas of life, the best approach is one of *moderation*. Encouraging moderate, balanced food intake and moderate amounts of regular physical activity should be helpful in promoting a healthy lifestyle both for overweight youngsters and for those young people who tend toward the excessive calorie restriction and extreme exercise that are associated with eating disorders.[88]

Stice agrees with this idea. He is interested in helping people with obesity problems and eating disorders and he believes that both conditions are just two sides of the same issue—a brain

Some experts say that anti-obesity campaigns, such as those conducted by the Department of Human Services, can backfire on people with a predisposition for an eating disorder.

disorder with faulty neurotransmitters that leads to an unhealthy relationship with food. Stice's Healthy Weight program, based on his study of interventions, emphasizes moderation and healthy eating, not diets. People in this program (whether binge eaters or not) learn to gradually reduce the least healthy foods that they eat (such as fast foods) while gradually increasing healthy food. They also learn to gradually increase exercise. They are taught the concept of balancing energy intake (calories) with energy needs.

Putting the program into practice is easy and painless. Every participant is asked at first to pick small things to change. For example, they might give up one bad food and add one small bit of extra physical activity. As time goes on, they may add other healthier choices, one step at a time. The intervention is supposed to be a permanent lifestyle change, never a diet. Stice explains, "Instead of saying, 'Eat 1,800 calories a day and exercise 35 minutes, seven days a week,' we just let the kids decide what they can do to improve their lifestyle, and it seem[s] to work very well."[89]

Stice believes that his Healthy Weight program and his Body Project program could prevent disordered eating by changing attitudes and behaviors while people are young. He says,

> One reason these programs might be more effective [than other prevention programs] is that they require youth to take a more healthy perspective, which leads them to internalize the more healthy attitudes. In addition, these programs have simple take-home messages, which may be easier to remember in the future than messages from more complex prevention programs. . . . It is our hope that other institutions and communities will adopt this program for delivery in their schools. If this program is delivered to enough youth, it should be possible to reduce the prevalence of these serious health problems.[90]

Protecting Oneself

Stice's work with eating disorders and obesity suggests that universal programs can change the unhealthy ways that people respond to food. It also provides evidence that teens can independently take charge of their own health and attitudes. The Center for Young Women's Health at Children's Hospital in Boston offers these tips to teens for staying healthy and developing a good body image:

- Identify and respect everything about yourself—the inside and the outside.

- Be yourself. Don't try to look like models in magazines.

- Try not to think or talk about weight, calories, and food.

- Try to make eating a positive experience: eating fuels both your body and mind!

- Don't diet! Try to eat mostly healthy foods.

- Work on ways to cope with negative feelings, such as talking to friends or family, listening to music, playing a sport, or doing crafts. Practicing healthy ways to deal with stress may help you avoid using food to deal with emotions.[91]

Social Change: Everyone Can Play a Part

The Center for Young Women's Health addresses the need to question society's standards as well. Although it speaks to young women, its words apply equally to young men who struggle with weight and body image. In addition, the advice is

Food Anonymous is just one of several eating disorder support groups available to those whose lives have been overtaken by the need to binge.

valuable for people who are not troubled by disordered eating but want to reject a culture that encourages eating disorders. The center says:

> It is important for us to look at our attitudes and behaviors in our own lives to help us understand how we can prevent eating disorders in our culture. Teasing and harassment about weight and body shape often leads young women to develop eating disordered behaviors. Conversations and activities that focus only on thinness, weight, and dieting can be harmful.
>
> Magazines and movies promote unrealistic role models for beauty and weight. Often, we are presented with an image that is unnaturally thin and unlike most women. It is important to realize that we are all meant to be different shapes and sizes and that pictures in magazines are airbrushed.
>
> The dieting industry also may push us to try and change our bodies into something we are not. Most young women have come to accept dieting as a part of growing up; yet dieting and restricting calories can cause serious psychological and physiological consequences such as the inability to focus at school, tiredness, and depression. Girls who diet actually are more likely to gain weight [than] those who don't diet.
>
> Accepting these unreasonable standards to measure bodies may create disordered thinking and behaviors and generally low self-esteem. It is very difficult to avoid or fight back against the industry that places these ideas in our head, but we can try. Together we can reverse the social environment and mind-set that creates eating disorders![92]

Introduction: It Is Not Just About Food

1. Something Fishy Website on Eating Disorders. www.some
thing-fishy.org.
2. Quoted in Something Fishy Website on Eating Disorders.
3. Something Fishy Website on Eating Disorders.

Chapter 1: The Problem of Eating Disorders

4. Barbara, "Another Mother's Story," Eating Disorders in a
Disordered Culture: Stories Told, University of California
at Davis, 1999. www.eating.ucdavis.edu/speaking/told/ff/f9
barbaraG.html.
5. Ben, "Ben, June 25th, 2000," Something Fishy Website on
Eating Disorders: Recovery Stories. www.something-fishy
.org/reach/otherside_ben.php.
6. National Institute of Mental Health, "Eating Disorders," February 11, 2009. www.nimh.nih.gov/health/publications/
eating-disorders/complete-index.shtml.
7. National Eating Disorders Association, "Anorexia Nervosa." www.nationaleatingdisorders.org/p.asp?WebPage_ID=
286&Profile_ID=41142.
8. Quoted in David B. Herzog, Debra L. Franko, and Pat Cable,
Unlocking the Mysteries of Eating Disorders. New York: McGraw-
Hill, 2008, p. 30.
9. Herzog, Franko, and Cable, *Unlocking the Mysteries of Eating
Disorders*, p. 34.
10. B. Timothy Walsh and V.L. Cameron, *If Your Adolescent
Has an Eating Disorder*. New York: Oxford University Press,
2005, p. 53.
11. Robert Levey, "Anorexia Nervosa: Overview," eMedicine
from WebMD, April 17, 2006. http://emedicine.medscape
.com/article/286063-overview.

12. Howard Markel, "CASES: Anorexia Can Strike Boys, Too," *New York Times*, July 25, 2000. www.nytimes.com/2000/07/25/health/cases-anorexia-can-strike-boys-too.html.

13. National Institute of Mental Health, "Eating Disorders."

14. Hayley, "Hayley's Story," Eating Disorders in a Disordered Culture: Stories Told: Bulimia Stories, University of California at Davis. www.eating.ucdavis.edu/speaking/told/bulimia/b77hayley.html.

15. Lindsey Hall and Leigh Cohn, *Bulimia: A Guide to Recovery*. Santa Barbara, CA: Gurze, 1986, pp. 39, 44.

16. National Eating Disorders Association, "Binge Eating Disorder." www.nationaleatingdisorders.org/p.asp?WebPage_ID=286&Profile_ID=41140.

17. "Tracey," Something Fishy Website on Eating Disorders: Personal Stories. www.something-fishy.org/whatarethey/coe_stories1.php.

18. Academy of Eating Disorders, "Prevalence of Eating Disorders." www.aedweb.org/eating_disorders/prevalence.cfm.

Chapter 2: The Causes of Eating Disorders

19. Quoted in Joseph A. Silverman, "History of Anorexia Nervosa," in Kelly D. Brownell and Christopher G. Fairburn, eds., *Eating Disorders and Obesity: A Comprehensive Handbook*. New York: Guilford, 1995, p. 141.

20. Quoted in Joan Jacobs Brumberg, *Fasting Girls*. Cambridge, MA: Harvard University Press, 1988, p. 10.

21. Brenda Parry-Jones and William L. Parry-Jones, "History of Bulimia and Bulimia Nervosa," in Kelly D. Brownell and Christopher G. Fairburn, eds., *Eating Disorders and Obesity*. New York: Guilford, 1995, p. 149.

22. Susan Nolen-Hoeksema, *Eating, Drinking, Overthinking: The Toxic Triangle of Food, Alcohol, and Depression—and How Women Can Break Free*. New York: Henry Holt, 2006, p. 98.

23. Walter H. Kaye, Guido K. Frank, Ursula F. Bailer, Shannan E. Henry, Carolyn C. Meltzer, Julie C. Price, Chester A. Mathis, and Angela Wagner, "Serotonin Alterations in

Anorexia and Bulimia Nervosa: New Insights from Imaging Studies," *Journal of Physiology and Behavior*, Vol 85, no. 1, May 19, 2005, p. 78.

24. Karl M. Pirke, "Physiology of Bulimia Nervosa," in Brownell and Fairburn, *Eating Disorders and Obesity*, p. 264.

25. University of Maryland Medical Center, "Eating Disorders—Causes," Patient Education. www.umm.edu/patiented/articles/what_causes_eating_disorders_000049_3.htm.

26. Quoted in Mary K. Stein, "New Directions and Challenges Ahead for Eating Disorders," *Eating Disorders Review*, vol. 18, no. 4, July/August 2007. www.gurze.com/client/client_pages/nl_edr_18_4.cfm.

27. Simona Giordano, *Understanding Eating Disorders*. New York: Oxford University Press, 2005, p. 84.

28. Rachel Marsh, Joanna E. Steinglass, Andrew J. Gerber, Kara Graziano O'Leary, Zhishun Wang, David Murphy, B. Timothy Walsh, and Bradley S. Peterson, "Deficient Activity in the Neural Systems That Mediate Self-Regulatory Control in Bulimia Nervosa," *Archives of General Psychiatry*, vol. 66, no. 1, January 2009, pp. 51–63. http://archpsyc.ama-assn.org/cgi/content/short/66/1/51.

29. Quoted in *Harvard University Gazette*, "Binge Eating Disorder May Have Genetic Ties, McLean Hospital Study Finds," Harvard Science, March 9, 2006. www.harvardscience.harvard.edu/medicine-health/articles/binge-eating-disorder-may-have-genetic-ties-mclean-hospital-study-finds.

30. Walsh and Cameron, *If Your Adolescent Has an Eating Disorder*, p. 37.

31. National Eating Disorders Association, "Causes of Eating Disorders." www.nationaleatingdisorders.org/p.asp?WebPage_ID=286&Profile_ID=41144.

32. Kathleen Mary Berg, Dermot J. Hurley, James A. McSherry, and Nancy E. Strange, *Eating Disorders: A Patient-Centered Approach*. Abingdon, UK: Radcliffe, 2002, p. 53.

33. Quoted in Marlene Busko and Penny Murata, "Childhood Sexual Abuse Linked with Bulimia in Later Life," Medscape

CME, March 6, 2008. http://cme.medscape.com/viewarticle/571082.

34. National Eating Disorders Association, "Causes of Eating Disorders."

35. Nolen-Hoeksema, *Eating, Drinking, Overthinking*, p. 85.

Chapter 3: Living with an Eating Disorders

36. Jane Shure and Beth Weinstock, "Shame, Compassion, and the Journey Toward Health," in Margo Maine, William N. Davis, and Jane Shure, eds., *Effective Clinical Practice in the Treatment of Eating Disorders*. New York: Routledge, 2009, p. 168.

37. Annaclaire, "Annaclaire's Story: Anorexia Nervosa," Eating Disorders in a Disordered Culture: Stories Told, University of California at Davis. www.eating.ucdavis.edu/speaking/told/anorexia/a35annaclaire.html.

38. Annaclaire, "Annaclaire's Story."

39. Annaclaire, "Annaclaire's Story."

40. Annaclaire, "Annaclaire's Story."

41. Annaclaire, "Annaclaire's Story."

42. Patrick Bergstrom, "A Fallen Athlete," I Chose to Live.com, p. 3. www.ichosetolive.com/files/A_Fallen_Athlete.pdf.

43. Bergstrom, "A Fallen Athlete," p. 5.

44. Bergstrom, "A Fallen Athlete," p. 12.

45. Bergstrom, "A Fallen Athlete," p. 16.

46. Patrick Bergstrom, "I Chose to Live," Stories of Hope, National Eating Disorders Association. www.nationaleating disorders.org/information-resources/story-of-hope-detail .php?story=5&title=I Chose to Live.

47. Quoted in Ira M. Sacker, *Regaining Your Self*. New York: Hyperion, 2007, pp. 36–37.

48. Allison, "My Story of ED," Stories of Hope, National Eating Disorders Association. www.nationaleatingdisorders .org/information-resources/story-of-hope-detail.php?story= 4&title=My Story of My ED.

49. Hall and Cohn, *Bulimia: A Guide to Recovery*, p. 39.

50. Hall and Cohn, *Bulimia: A Guide to Recovery*, p. 36.

51. Hall and Cohn, *Bulimia: A Guide to Recovery*, p. 43.

52. Jean, "From Jean," Personal Stories: Compulsive Overeating, Something Fishy.org. www.something-fishy.org/what arethey/coe_stories1.php.

53. Jean, "From Jean."

54. Liz, "From Liz," Personal Stories: Compulsive Overeating, Something Fishy.org. www.something-fishy.org/what arethey/coe_stories1.php.

55. Liz, "From Liz."

56. Jennifer, "Jennifer's Story: San Jose, California, Compulsive Eating," Eating Disorders in a Disordered Culture: Stories Told, University of California at Davis. www.eating.ucdavis .edu/speaking/told/compuls/jennifer.html.

57. Quoted in Raina Seitel Gittlin, "Male Binge Eating: One Man's Courageous Story," Health, ABC News, February 25, 2007. http://abcnews.go.com/GMA/Health/Story?id= 2901805&page=1.

Chapter 4: The Diagnosis and Treatment of Eating Disorders

58. Quoted in Kathleen N. Franco, "Eating Disorders," Disease Management Project, Cleveland Clinic Center for Continuing Education. www.clevelandclinicmeded.com/medical pubs/diseasemanagement/psychiatry/eating-disorders.

59. Quoted in Franco, "Eating Disorders."

60. Quoted in Franco, "Eating Disorders."

61. Quoted in Lifespan, "Inadequate Diagnostic Criteria for Eating Disorders, Study Shows," *Science Daily*, February 6, 2008. www.sciencedaily.com/releases/2008/02/080206090457 .htm.

62. Something Fishy Website on Eating Disorders, "Eating Disorder Not Otherwise Specified (ED-NOS)." www.some thing-fishy.org/whatarethey/ednos.php.

63. Walsh and Cameron, *If Your Adolescent Has an Eating Disorder*, pp. 68–69.

64. Herzog, Franko, and Cable, *Unlocking the Mysteries of Eating Disorders*, p. 69.

65. Quoted in Walsh and Cameron, *If Your Adolescent Has an Eating Disorder*, p. 129.

66. Quoted in Herzog, Franko, and Cable, *Unlocking the Mysteries of Eating Disorders*, p. 127.

67. Ira M. Sacker, *Regaining Your Self*. New York: Hyperion, 2007, p. 3.

68. Bergstrom, "A Fallen Athlete," pp. 22–23.

69. Quoted in Herzog, Franko, and Cable, *Unlocking the Mysteries of Eating Disorders*, p. 70.

70. Quoted in Herzog, Franko, and Cable, *Unlocking the Mysteries of Eating Disorders*, p. 70.

71. Quoted in Herzog, Franko, and Cable, *Unlocking the Mysteries of Eating Disorders*, pp. 70–71.

72. Quoted in Herzog, Franko, and Cable, *Unlocking the Mysteries of Eating Disorders*, p. 153.

73. Sacker, *Regaining Your Self*, p. 184.

74. Sacker, *Regaining Your Self*, p. 186.

75. Herzog, Franko, and Cable, *Unlocking the Mysteries of Eating Disorders*, p. 81.

76. Herzog, Franko, and Cable, *Unlocking the Mysteries of Eating Disorders*, p. 98.

Chapter 5: Tackling the Larger Issue: Prevention of Eating Disorders

77. Walsh and Cameron, *If Your Adolescent Has an Eating Disorder*, p. 133.

78. Walsh and Cameron, *If Your Adolescent Has an Eating Disorder*, p. 136.

79. Quoted in Chuck Staresinic, "Refusing Sustenance: In Search of Earthly Explanations for Eating Disorders," PittMed, May 2004, p. 15. www.wpic.pitt.edu/research/angenetics/press/cover_story.pdf.

80. Basque Research: News, "Emotions Can Help Predict Future Eating Disorders," March 17, 2009. www.basqueresearch.com/berria_irakurri.asp?Berri_Kod=2124&hizk=I.

81. Eric Stice, C. Nathan Marti, Sonja Spoor, Katherine Presnell, and Heather Shaw, "Dissonance and Healthy Weight Eating Disorder Prevention Programs: Long-Term Effects from a Randomized Efficacy Trial," *Journal of Consulting and Clinical Psychology*, vol. 76, no. 2, p. 329, 2008. http://foodaddiction summit.org/docs/SticeMarti2008.pdf.

82. Stice et al., "Dissonance and Healthy Weight Eating Disorder Prevention Programs," pp. 332–33.

83. Quoted in Sanjay Gupta, "Taking on the Thin Ideal," *House Calls: Fit Nation*, CNN/*Time* Magazine. www.time.com/ time/specials/2007/article/0,28804,1703763_1703764_ 1810730,00.html.

84. Reflections Body Image Program, "The Program." www .bodyimageprogram.org/program.

85. Reflections Body Image Program, "Upcoming Events." www .bodyimageprogram.org/action/events.

86. Frances M. Berg, "Prevention Programs for Obesity and Related Problems," *Healthy Weight Journal*, vol. 15, no. 4, July/August 2001, p. 62. www.gurze.net/HAESprotected/ HAES15-4.pdf.

87. Walsh and Cameron, *If Your Adolescent Has an Eating Disorder*, pp. 140–41.

88. Walsh and Cameron, *If Your Adolescent Has an Eating Disorder*, pp. 146–47.

89. Quoted in Jennifer Winters, "Researchers Stumble on Obesity Prevention," KVAL.com, May 8, 2008. www.kval.com/ news/health/18768359.html.

90. Quoted in Mohit Joshi, "Body Image Program Cuts Obesity Onset, Eating Disorders Risk," TopNews Health, April 30, 2008. www.topnews.in/health/body-image-program-cuts-obesity-onset-eating-disorders-risk-22234.

91. Center for Young Women's Health, "Eating Disorders: A General Guide for Teens," Children's Hospital Boston. www .youngwomenshealth.org/eating_disorders.html.

92. Center for Young Women's Health, "Eating Disorders: A General Guide for Teens."

Chapter 1: The Problem of Eating Disorders

1. How are eating disorders different from diets or unhealthy eating?

2. How are anorexia, bulimia, and binge eating disorder similar and how are they different?

3. What behaviors and symptoms might be warning signs that someone has an eating disorder?

Chapter 2: The Causes of Eating Disorders

1. What are some possible reasons that more females than males succumb to eating disorders?

2. How do genetics and environment interact to cause eating disorders?

3. How does cultural pressure make people dissatisfied with their appearance?

Chapter 3: Living with an Eating Disorders

1. What are some of the different risk factors that trigger eating disorders?

2. How do friends and family influence the course of eating disorders?

3. How are food and feelings connected?

Chapter 4: The Diagnosis and Treatment of Eating Disorders

1. What are the problems and issues with diagnostic methods today?

2. What is the Maudsley method and why is it a good treatment approach?

3. What are the benefits of residential treatment versus outpatient treatment?

Chapter 5: Tackling the Larger Issue: Prevention of Eating Disorders

1. What are some of the benefits of early diagnosis?

2. How are body image and self-esteem affected by society, peer pressure, and the media?

3. What are some examples of fat talk and why might avoiding such talk help prevent eating disorders?

ORGANIZATIONS TO CONTACT

Academy for Eating Disorders (AED)
60 Revere Dr., Ste. 500
Northbrook, IL 60062
phone: (847) 498-4274
Web site: www.aed.org

AED is a professional organization that emphasizes prevention and research.

A Chance to Heal
PO Box 2342
Jenkintown, PA 19046
phone: (215) 885-2420
Web site: http://achancetoheal.org

This is a nonprofit organization dedicated to raising awareness of and public education about eating disorders. It also offers financial assistance to individuals unable to pay for appropriate treatment.

Eating Disorder Referral and Information Center
2923 Sandy Pointe, Ste. 6
Del Mar, CA 92014
phone: (858) 481-1515
Web site: www.edreferral.com

This organization provides an extensive and searchable database about where and how to get treatment for eating disorders. It answers questions about treatment and prevention of eating disorders.

National Eating Disorders Association (NEDA)
603 Stewart St., Ste. 103
Seattle, WA 98101

phone (toll-free help line): (800) 931-2237

Web site: www.nationaleatingdisorders.org

NEDA provides education, resources, and support for those affected by eating disorders and their friends and family.

National Institute of Mental Health (NIMH)

6001 Executive Blvd., Room 8184 MSC 9663

Bethesda, MD 20892

phone: (866) 615-6464

Web site: www.nimh.nih.gov.

NIMH offers a wide selection of informational publications about eating disorders.

FOR MORE INFORMATION

Books

Lauri S. Friedman and Jennifer L. Skancke, eds., *Introducing Issues with Opposing Viewpoints: Eating Disorders*. Farmington Hills, MI: Greenhaven, 2008. A series of articles helps readers critically examine the emerging science of eating disorders. Differing viewpoints on the causes, prevention, and treatment of eating disorders are presented.

Tammy Nelson, *What's Eating You? A Workbook for Teens with Anorexia, Bulimia, and Other Eating Disorders*. Oakland, CA: Instant Help, 2008. Through a series of activities, this book helps people understand and question the underlying issues that support their eating disorder and build the strength to overcome their poor body images and disordered relationships with food.

Tamra B. Orr, *When the Mirror Lies: Anorexia, Bulimia, and Other Eating Disorders*. Danbury, CT: Franklin Watts, 2007. This book describes the pain of living with eating disorders, discusses the attitudes and behaviors that trigger the illnesses, and suggests how to prevent them.

Nadia Shivack, *Inside Out: Portrait of an Eating Disorder*. New York: Atheneum/Ginee Seo, 2007. The author writes about and illustrates her journey toward recovery from her eating disorder.

Scott Simon, *Male Bulimia: My Dark Demon*. Lincoln, NE: iUniverse, 2006. The author describes his personal battle with an eating disorder and how, after many years, he was able to overcome the demon and recover.

Gail Stewart, *Health at Risk: Anorexia*. Ann Arbor, MI: Cherry Lake, 2008. In this easy-to-read book, the author explains anorexia and helps readers to think critically about this serious illness.

Web Sites

Adios Barbie (www.adiosbarbie.com). The goal of this Web site is to encourage young women to reject the idea of a perfect, Barbie-doll body and learn to love themselves the way they are.

"Food and Fitness," TeensHealth for Teens (http://kidshealth .org/teen/food_fitness). Articles describe the healthy way to choose a diet, exercise, be fit, and develop a good body image. In the link "Problems with Food and Exercise," visitors can learn about eating disorders and how athletes can cope with exercise and the demands of sports without resorting to negative behaviors.

"Pageant Pants," H.O.P.E. (Helping Other People Eat) (www .hopetolive.com/pagpants.html). Allison Kreiger, Miss Florida 2006 and in recovery from bulimia, began a campaign in conjunction with the Miss Florida Pageant to give away donated pairs of jeans and raise awareness and money for the prevention of eating disorders. Visitors to this site can learn about the drive to help everyone "feel comfortable in your genes."

Something Fishy (www.something-fishy.org). This is a recovery Web site for anyone who is touched by an eating disorder. Extensive information, stories of hope, and discussion forums are just part of the available resources.

INDEX

PICTURE CREDITS

Cover: © Jim Zuckerman/Alamy

Anwar Hussein/WireImage/Getty Images, 23

AP Images, 37, 47, 88, 90

© [apply pictures]/Ralf Mohr/Alamy, 45

BSIP/Photo Researchers, Inc., 83

© Bubbles Photolibrary/Alamy, 7, 25, 57

Carolyn A. McKeone/Photo Researchers, Inc., 72

Claus Lunau/Bonnier Publications/Photo Researchers, Inc., 35

© David J. Green/Alamy, 62

© David J. Green—Lifestyle/Alamy, 20

David Mack/Photo Researchers, Inc., 32

Ethan Miller/Getty Images, 51

Fred Prouser/Reuters/Landov, 49

Gary O'Brien/MCT/Landov, 60

Health Protection Agency/Photo Researchers, Inc., 77

Oscar Burriel/Photo Researchers, Inc., 10, 40, 80

Simon Fraser/Photo Researchers, Inc., 18

SSPL/Getty Images, 28

© Steve Skjold/Alamy, 70

Steve Zmina/Gale, Cengage Learning, 16, 22

Susan Rosenberg/Photo Researchers, Inc., 13

Taro Yamasaki/Time Life Pictures/Getty Images, 67

© www.Beepstock.com/Robinbeckham/Alamy, 42

ABOUT THE AUTHOR

Toney Allman holds a BS in psychology from Ohio State University and an MA in clinical psychology from the University of Hawaii. She currently lives in Virginia and writes books for students on a variety of topics.